Lauren,

Thanks so much for your
support! Hope you enjoy
the book!

4/13/19

The Strange Case of Dr. Jekyll and Mr. Hyde by Robert Louis Stevenson (1886) is a classic piece of fiction that is still read and studied one hundred years after being written. *Thomas Sweatt: Inside the Mind of DC's Most Notorious Arsonist* by Jonathan E. Riffe is a true story, told in the first person, of possibly the most prolific arsonist in American history.

Thanks to Jonathan, and the arsonist who fell in love with him, readers and researchers have the opportunity to glimpse into the thoughts of Tom Sweatt, who set fires and murdered people for twenty years.

The research value of the thousands of pages of original documentation is yet to be determined, but the fields of crime-scene investigation, forensic psychology, and criminal-behavior profiling has a treasure trove of material that will impact the study and investigation of arson for decades.

It's common knowledge that firefighters are brave. We run into burning buildings—being brave is the easy part of the job and it is fun. We all live for the excitement and the admiration from the public. Lieutenant Riffe is taking a one of a kind risk with this book that is beyond anything firefighters are taught in rookie school or encounter throughout their careers. He has walked into a world we do not go publicly—arson and homosexuality.

When you read a novel, you do not know the end. We know the ending of true stories. In this book, you will read about the who, what, when, where, why, and how of arson and murder, law and order, philological deviance, crime and punishment, and the terror of fire. All caused by one man.

After you read this book, you will want more. I did. So I made Jonathan promise me two tickets to the world movie premiere and best-seller book party.

To all the readers, from a former District of Columbia and Prince George's County firefighter—hello and what's up. Creepy!

DR. BURTON A. CLARK, EFO

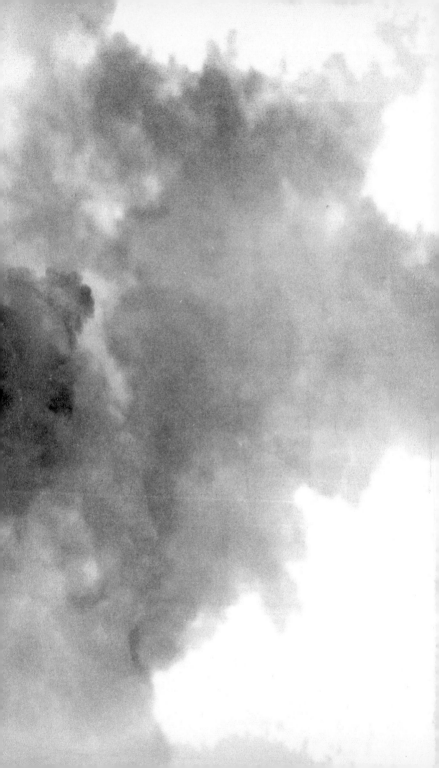

Praise for
Thomas Sweatt

"Just finished reading the new release *Thomas Sweatt: Inside the Mind of DC's Most Notorious Arsonist.* In a word, this book is AMAZING. Chief Jonathan Riffe has provided an insight like nothing else that I have read. Jon captures the reader's imagination as he shares his years of research communicating with Thomas Sweatt, perhaps this nation's most prolific arsonist. A tip of the helmet to the Chief for his significant contribution to our body of knowledge and our understanding about the mission critical topic of understanding the motivation of a serial arsonist. Add a copy of this powerful book to your personal and departmental library today!"

-Chief Dennis Rubin

www.mascotbooks.com

Thomas Sweatt: Inside the Mind of DC's Most Notorious Arsonist
©2018 Jonathan Riffe. All Rights Reserved. No part of this publication may be reproduced, stored in a retrieval system or transmitted in any form by any means electronic, mechanical, or photocopying, recording or otherwise without the permission of the author.

Some names and identifying details have been changed to protect the privacy of individuals.

For more information, please contact:
Mascot Books
620 Herndon Parkway, Suite 320
Herndon, VA 20170
info@mascotbooks.com

Library of Congress Control Number: 2017913781

CPSIA Code: PBANG1117A
ISBN-13: 978-1-68401-626-6

Printed in the United States

THOMAS SWEATT

INSIDE THE MIND
OF
DC'S MOST NOTORIOUS ARSONIST

Jonathan Riffe

The serial arsonist is the most difficult to apprehend because the evidence is burned up.

—JOSEPH WAMBAUGH

Foreword

This is an amazing book about the most prolific serial arsonist in history. Thomas Sweatt, an African American homosexual, was arrested and eventually confessed to over 340 arson-set fires, which all told killed four people. He committed these crimes in the area in and around Washington, DC. I have been a firefighter for fifty-five years and have come directly in contact with arson as a street firefighter, and I've been responsible as a fire chief for managing an arson investigation, apprehension, and conviction program, but the frequency and severity of his crimes go way beyond my frame of reference or imagination.

Another amazing part of this book is how the story has been assembled by Jonathan Riffe. Jon is a very capable, well educated, and experienced fire officer. He serves as the fire chief of a busy suburban volunteer fire department, and he is also a company officer in the District of Columbia Fire and Emergency Medical Services Department. He routinely manages a fire department on an executive level as a fire chief and serves as the boss of a fire company in a busy big city fire department, where he routinely encounters and resolves just about every fire and emergency medical problem that comes with a complicated, densely populated, and diverse city. He developed an interest in the string of arsonist fires that occurred right where he works and lives.

He communicated with the arsonist and then developed a very special relationship with him. They talked by phone and mail where the details of the fire setting were relayed to and recorded by Jon. He provided some ongoing financial assistance both to support purchasing communications material (paper, envelopes, postage, etc.) and to get incidentals to the arsonist inside the prison. In a very skillful way, Jon created a personal relationship and established a deep level of trust with the arsonist. It's obviously challenging to capture a criminal's own voice when the details of a complicated story are conveyed in a removed way by phone and mail. It seems to me that Jon could be a very capable detective, as he has the natural skill and resourcefulness to relate to a criminal so they will open up and tell their own story—and what an unbelievable story it is.

A huge part of this case was the fire-setting skill of the arsonist. During my career, I have been a continual student of evaluating the critical factors on the fire ground—or the scene of the fire—that become the basis for putting the fire out. We call this process "sizing up." This evaluation becomes the basis for establishing an overall fire-control operational strategy and the related incident action plan. When I read this book, I was fascinated by the size-up skill of the arsonist to develop an incident action plan to set (not extinguish) the fire. He used the same physical and environmental critical factors we use on the extinguishment side to influence how he set the fire on the arson side. I have never contemplated how powerful those conditions would be for a criminal to initiate a fire that we are then trying to extinguish.

He clearly understood that a fire can begin as a very private affair for the arsonist and can then quickly grow into a very public event. He developed his own critical size-up factors that related to when, where, and how he set a fire, and the number of fires he set is astonishing. The contrasting characteristic of fire origin and growth is that it can start on a microscopic level and then (sometimes very quickly) evolve into a monstrous size.

He understood the local conditions where he could come and go undetected and leave a burning structure behind him and confound the arson investigators over and over. This detached mobility creates the opportunity for the fire setter to be very unobtrusive in setting the fire before moving to a safe spot and becoming a fire spectator. This mean, sneaky act leaves the victims behind to deal with being assaulted, and sometimes killed, by the fire. It is simply a lot easier for the arsonist to escape than for those who the fire surprises and sometimes captures. While he was very skillful in not getting caught, he was also very low tech. He basically set his fires with a small jug of gasoline and a sock(!). He quietly transported his arson stuff in a plastic shopping bag, so he just looked like he was carrying groceries—simple but very effective. He had the mobility and concealment advantage of being able to move around the community freely and hide in the dark.

It is amazing that he was able to continue his fire-setting spree for so long based on where he did it. The Washington, DC, metropolitan area is protected by the most advanced and progressive fire and police departments in the world. On the fire side, there is virtually a fire station every mile, staffed by the most experienced and capable firefighters anywhere. The author of this book is among that group of pros. On the police side, there are dozens of separate police departments protecting the Capitol area; more than anywhere else on earth—in fact, the headquarters of all the national-level law enforcement agencies are literally in the shadow of where the fires were set. While he confounded these public protection folks (fire/police) for a long time, they did their usual patient, methodical process and finally closed in on him.

A major reason for his longevity as an arsonist was that he was in no way personally connected to the places where he set fires or those who were affected by the fires. Generally, arson is associated with fires set for profit, fires set to conceal crimes, or fires started out of spite based on dysfunctional relationships. When these causes are present, cops have the ability (and skill) to gain background knowledge through investigation. Simply, in these cases there is something for them "to get their teeth in." In this case, the arsonist did not have any connection to the people, places, or things he set on fire. Literally, he strolled around, sized up a likely structure, set it on fire, and disappeared. For him to be detected only depended on someone seeing or catching him in the act, and most of the people in that very local area who could do that were asleep. But in this case (as usual), the cops will win regardless of how skillful the criminal is.

What you are about to read is truly an amazing story.

FIRE CHIEF ALAN BRUNACINI

Contents

Introduction

In 1996, I joined the Huntingtown Volunteer Fire Department, located in Calvert County, Maryland, at the young age of sixteen. I slowly moved through the ranks until I became fire chief in 2007, where I served in that capacity for six years. I quickly realized that I had found my calling and began to devote all my time and energy into making this a full-time career. In 1999, I was hired as a federal firefighter with the Naval District Washington Fire Department. I remained there until the beginning of 2004, when I resigned and went to work with the United States Capitol Police Hazardous Materials Response Team. After a short tenure there, I received the phone call I had been waiting for. The District of Columbia Fire Department offered me a job, which I graciously accepted. I began the training academy on August 9, 2004. I was later promoted to sergeant on July 17, 2011, and then lieutenant on October 6, 2013.

During my fifteen-week period in the training academy as a recruit, a vicious manhunt was in effect for a deadly serial arsonist who was sweeping across the streets of Washington, DC, Prince George's County, Maryland, Montgomery County, Maryland, and Northern Virginia, undetected like a ghost. While in the training academy, the fifty-one recruits took field trips on DC Fire Department buses to the neighborhoods that the serial arsonist had torched, knocking door-to-door, inspecting and installing smoke detectors. His path of destruction was unimaginable. How long would this deadly and destructive rampage continue?

I've taken many classes through the years studying the science of fire behavior. The nature and behavior of fire has always been intriguing to me. Fire seems to fascinate everyone, whether this fascination stems from admiration or fear. For some, though, fire can be used in an evil and destructive manner. In 2005, the identity of the arsonist was revealed and Thomas Sweatt was arrested. He eventually confessed to over 340 arsons, which ultimately killed four people (that investigators are certain of, at least). He was charged and convicted with the most counts of arson in the history of the United States. Because Mr. Sweatt had been undetected and untouched for a period of twenty-five years, investigators have named him the "most prolific and dangerous serial arsonist in American history." He was found guilty on fifteen counts, eleven counts to be served concurrently. The other sentences are to be served consecutive to those eleven counts, independent of one another. Thus, the longest initial sentence of 262 months will be followed by the thirty-year sentence, then the sixty-year sentence, the 288-month sentence, and finally the life sentence. Mr. Sweatt was committed on September 12, 2005, to the custody of the United States Federal Bureau of Prisons to be imprisoned for a total term of life, consecutive to a term of 1,630 months.

The stereotypical profile of a serial arsonist is a young white male. Tom, however, was an older African American homosexual. His life intrigued me. Who was he? Why did he do it? How did he do it? I wanted to know all the whats, whys, whos, whens, wheres, and hows of the story and everything about his deadly and destructive life. Unfortunately, after his arrest and conviction, I never heard anything else about him.

In exchange for his guilty plea with prosecutors, he asked for and received a promise of confidentiality, forever locking away his motives for the fires. I waited patiently for several years for a book to be published or movie to be made about his underground life. Once a major criminal is captured, it usually doesn't take long for a book to be published or a movie to be released describing the individual's life. However, that never occurred. In April 2011, I made a decision that I was confident would be pointless and of no value. I researched him online and found that he was serving his sentence at the Federal Correctional Complex in Coleman, Florida. The following letter was sent on April 18, 2011:

Mr. Sweatt,

My name is Jonathan Riffe. I am a firefighter in Washington, DC, where I have been employed for the past seven years. I work at 30 Engine, which is on Forty-Ninth Street NE. I am also the chief of the Huntingtown VFD (in Southern Maryland) where I have volunteered for the past fifteen years. I write articles for national magazines such as Fire Engineering and Firehouse (not sure if you are familiar).

I have a bachelor of science degree in fire science. Fire behavior intrigues me, as you could possibly imagine. I have read about your fires for several years and wondered if anybody has ever approached you about writing a book. If not, I would most definitely like to begin working on this. Let me know your thoughts, and I look forward to hearing from you.

Regards,

Jonathan Riffe

Was I crazy? I had just written a letter to a killer serving two consecutive life sentences. I had never written a book before! I was unaware of the doors I had just opened and what I was about to get myself into. I knew the letter would be fruitless, and I suspected that I would never hear back from Mr. Sweatt. I learned of and read about countless authors, reporters, movie producers, etc., who had tried to contact and interview him. He refused everyone. I knew I would be unsuccessful. Two days later, I received a collect phone call on my cell phone from the prison. It was Tom, and I could hear his voice! It brought goose bumps and chills to my entire body. Unfortunately, because my cell phone was not registered as one of his contacts, I was unable to accept the phone call, which devastated me.

On April 24, 2011, six days after my initial letter, I received my first letter from Mr. Sweatt. During the next few years, several hundred letters, emails, and daily phone calls were exchanged. With every letter, I would enclose six pictures of random things that he admired (six photographs are the maximum amount he could receive in envelope). During my research, I was able to dig up all the court records (hundreds of pages) and speak with a few of the past investigators (the majority would not speak due to a gag order), past witnesses, and past firefighters. Mr. Sweatt mailed me a visitor information form (that only he could mail). I sent it back, but the US Federal Bureau of Prisons never accepted it.

Tom mentioned in several letters that I was honest, genuine, caring, and a true friend. Communicating with him via telephone, email, and letters quickly proved expensive. Weekly, I would have to send funds via Western Union, as the telephone calls, emails, paper, envelopes, postage, and writing utensils required money which he didn't have. Additionally, I sent extra funds for him to go to the vending machines and purchase extra items at the commissary. With this money, he was able to purchase a new radio, nice shoes, and many other things he normally wouldn't have the funds to purchase.

Under Thomas Sweatt's agreement with the government, investigators have been gagged from discussing Sweatt's motives or certain fires he may have admitted to during questioning. The information in this book is from the years of correspondence between the two of us and my own research. To protect certain individuals' identities, several names have been omitted.

Sweatt's untold story would have been swept away with time. This book came together by combing through several hundred letters and court transcripts. Behind the mask of this crazy, perverted, demented, killer serial arsonist is Thomas Sweatt, an African American homosexual loner in his late fifties who worked at various fast-food joints throughout his lifetime, and who turned Washington, DC, upside down into a living hell.

Tom Sweatt's Opening Statement:

I always enjoyed using fire as a tool—it gave me the power to destroy. The raging orange balls of fire and the dark smoke is truly a sight to see. As I watch people scramble to exit doors and windows, I felt as if they needed my help, so I would just stay and watch. I would masturbate over the fire while driving away from the scene and thinking about my next fire.

Chapter 1

THE START OF TOM SWEATT

My name is Thomas Anthony Sweatt, nickname "Peele." I'm called "Peele" because I'm the seventh child from the oldest, but I had a sister named Amanda Peele who would have been the sixth child had she lived. She was only ten days old. When I was born, my mother said I looked like Amanda. I was born November 1, 1954, at Roanoke Rapids Hospital in Roanoke Rapids, North Carolina, to Dozen Allen and Timothy Sweatt. (My father, Timothy, died in 2003.) My parents were married and had eleven children. (Author's note: Tom Sweatt's mother unfortunately passed away in 2012 while he and I were writing this book.)

I still remember that little house we lived in on White Street. You could see straight through it. There was an old, black wood stove that my mother used to make whole cake bread, which is just a biscuit in a black iron frying pan. She used to toss it in the air to flip it over to brown the other side. There was a line of the same style houses (shacks) on White Street. I remember there was a church on the other side of the street, which held about fifty people or so. The next street over was Pine Street, where we as children hung out. There was Sea Brewers Café and Johnny Garner's Barber Shop (where I paid 50 cents for a haircut). Mr. Garner was a tall, handsome man with big lips. When he cut my hair, I would be nervous and try to act as masculine as possible. I liked how his stomach would rub against my head. I pretended to know about sports when he talked about it. He's one of the men in North Carolina I would think about while masturbating.

There was a pool hall right beside the barber shop. My Uncle Howard and my brothers Patrick and Howard frequented there. That was not my style. So we knew exactly where to find one another on Friday and Saturday nights. My parents were poor, so we didn't have a lot of toys. One year, my daddy bought us a red bicycle for Christmas. All five of us boys had to take turns riding this bike! Even my sisters wanted to ride. That's pitiful, right? But we never went hungry.

I liked school and hated when I got sick. I suffered from a sore throat every year. First through fifth grade I did at Chaloner High School. Sixth through twelfth grade I did at the White School uptown, when schools were integrated in 1967–1968. I did average in school but had to study hard! I was mischievous and sneaky, but for some reason I got away. I stole ten dollars from my mother's pocket book. My oldest brother was blamed and got a whipping. I played with my sister's paper dolls and the Raggedy Ann dolls when they were away. I liked my mother's high heel shoes and would pretend to be a lady while the bedroom door was closed. When we would play house, I'd pretend to be the lady next door and be called Miss Lady and would answer in a feminine voice. I don't remember having a lot of friends because they were not allowed to come inside or hang around the house. I played pick-up basketball and baseball games in the field away from the house and on the back street, which was also a row of shacks.

My parents believed in God and were faithful Christians. We had meetings in the home. Our little house would be packed. The singing was pretty, but as a child growing up, the testimonies were too long and we got antsy. I professed in the church but only because of others. It really wasn't in my heart. I went to church. But the church was our home where I lived. My parents made us get up on Sunday mornings and attend the meetings. Our religion was (or is) nondenominational. We believe in the truth and God. We didn't worship in churches. We'd have bible studies every Wednesday and gospel meeting in nearby towns when the workers (ministers) would come around.

Most of my childhood was spent roaming through the woods, making straw houses, and picking blackberries. As children, we would sit on the front porch and count the cars coming and going in both directions. Whoever counted the most cars headed in their direction won. Our house was on a highway (Highway 158) and there was a good little amount of traffic. We'd all pile up in my daddy's car and go to Tastee Freez for their famous hot dogs and chocolate-dipped ice cream cone. We'd get the full-dress hot dogs with homemade coleslaw, chili, mustard, and ketchup. Then we'd drive around town looking at other people's cars, houses, and yards. Everyone knew everybody. People waved at strangers. I loved to eat at Rose's Dime Store and McCory's—they too had good hot dogs. I stole a nice-size white baby doll out of that store and walked with it all the way home. Two houses down from mine was a big old house with a long porch. The lady was old, and her mind was going. She'd go to bed at sundown and board up the doors before she went to sleep. I would sneak over to her house and give her 25 cents to play her piano. Then I'd steal her tablecloths and silverware. She loved to smoke.

My father beat us with the buckle of the belt, which gave us welts on our faces and bodies. He'd hold our heads between his knees and beat us with his belt or a tree switch. My mother would sometimes watch and tell him to stop, "That's enough" or "He's going to kill the poor child." My father was extremely abusive to my mother during my childhood up to my teenage years. They were the only parents I ever knew. Our father never showed love or kindness. He often called me a "he she" or a sissy. I just stood there and kept silent. My uncle came to our house one day and saw me standing in the kitchen. He said, "Oh... so he's gonna be one of them things?!" He had gold front teeth and worked with the race horses. He too had nice shoes, and I used to sit at the kitchen table and masturbate while thinking about him.

My parents stayed together for many years but eventually separated off and on throughout their later years. My mother worked in the cotton fields when I was little. I remembered going to pick cotton with her and got paid 50 cents for the whole day! Then she did cleaning for rich white folks for a while until finally getting a regular job as a sewer for J.P. Stevens Company, where she finally retired. My father rode a bike to work at the Rosemary Elementary School, where he worked as a janitor. As years passed, he landed a better-paying job at the Citizens Bank.

My brother Luther McKinley Sweatt was killed by my uncle Howard (on my daddy's side). My grandma (Rosella Sweatt) had three sons: Timothy, Moses, and Howard. My uncle Howard was living in my grandma's house, which was next to my daddy's house. Our house was yellow shingle and her house was green shingle. In 1979, my daddy and uncle had an argument of some sort in my uncle's house. My daddy went next door to his house and got my brother to help him fight my uncle. When they both went back to my uncle's house, my uncle stabbed my brother in the temple. He stumbled out of the kitchen door and went outside only to fall in the driveway near the wheel of the car. Had they got help sooner, I think my brother may have lived. He bled to death. They kept telling him to get up! Get up!

I had taken interest in cooking and hung around my grandmother (Ma Sweatt) because she was an excellent cook. To this day, there hasn't been a person to beat her cooking. During my teenage years was when I really learned how to cook. My family tried to keep me out of the kitchen, but my father always fought back and said, "Leave him alone and let him learn!" I became a very good cook :)!

I loved the water and can swim, but I've never been to the beach. I owned a pair of swimming trunks. They were white. I was baptized in them in a pond. Back in the day, my waist was twenty-eight inches. It's now forty inches. That's crazy. But I liked to wear tight clothes, and now I guess middle age has arrived :)! But I still got it going on. You dig?

I thought I was normal during my childhood, but as I grew older things just didn't seem right. I recall playing with books of matches—the old-fashioned kind. They came in a box of ten or twelve books. The match itself had a little red head on it, and you had to strike it real hard. My brothers and I used to wander off in the woods near our house to go play. We would "play house." We'd build a house made of straw (which would be the pine that fell from the tree) to cover the tree limbs. When we were finished, it would look something like a hut. Then we'd crawl under it and pretend to sleep for a while. Then we'd get tired and leave. But before leaving, I just had to set it on fire. I remember liking to set trash cans, dumpsters, etc., on fire and stand and stare at it.

I don't have a military background. I tried to enlist in the navy after high school, in 1973. I went to the recruiter's station and sat down with the recruiter. We talked. I took the test and passed it. I had to go to Raleigh, North Carolina, for a physical and was told I was hypertensive but to come back in six months. I said forget it. I knew how to swim, so I wasn't afraid to be out at sea. Plus, the blue and white sailor uniforms were sexy. I had two brothers who joined the army, and I wanted to be different.

I never had a desire to be a firefighter or police officer. In a small town like where I grew up, there was only one fire station and one police station at the same location. So there were not a lot of jobs in that area. When a fire truck would sound its siren, we'd get scared and the dogs would make a crying-like sound.

While living in Roanoke Rapids, I began to have this thing for hitchhikers. In 1972–1973, I had a pretty, blue 1969 Pontiac GTO. Our house was five to ten minutes away from Interstate 95, so it wasn't nothing to just get in the car and suddenly be on the highway. There was a lot of hitchhiking in the 70s and 80s because things were relatively safe. College students hiked their way to and from school. The hippie look was the thing, and faded blue jeans, long hair, and beards were sexy to me back then. Anyway, I knew if I took the exit to go up on I-95, someone would be standing right there at the mouth of the interstate. I could see them sometimes heading up the ramp off us Highway 158 (the road that we would travel through the city and on to Weldon and Halifax). So one night I took the keys and drove my brother's car to I-95 and saw this white man standing with a green fatigue–color bag, thumbing for a ride. I forget where he was going, but it was a long way away! I wasn't going too far either maybe a few miles—just enough to get to know him a little better and see where he's coming from. I pulled over. He got in the car and placed his bag in the back seat. I loved his heavy, wild voice. That was a start. I asked where he was going and he replied. But the devil started to take over my feelings, and I couldn't shake it off. The devil told me to take him down a dirt road and have sex with him.

Well, part of it happened, but things didn't go as planned. I took the exit, found the dirt road where there was no traffic, and pulled into some bushes. I turned the engine off and started to rub my fingers through his hair. For real, I don't know what I was doing to be honest—just experimenting. He said, "I'm heterosexual." I didn't know what that meant, either. I kissed his forehead. He didn't resist. But I started grabbing at his boots because they turned me on—the sound they made when he moved. Whatever I was doing it felt good to me. He just sat there and said he wanted to go. He got out of the car, and I asked him to push the car back onto the road. It was my plan to run him over. Instead, I got stuck. He did help me get out of the ditch and get back to the road. Then he started walking back to the highway. I didn't bother him anymore. Picking up hitchhikers became a part-time hobby of mine during high school.

There were also some sexy mail carriers who used to deliver the mail to our neighborhood. My mother was sewing a garment at the table in the kitchen one afternoon and decided to get up and found me in the living room door masturbating as the mailman approached our house. I was so embarrassed, but she never mentioned anything about it. She knew what I was doing.

Yes, I was deprived of being myself, having to live for others and not for Tom. I was scolded and told to have a girlfriend, to sit a certain way in a chair, to wear tennis shoes because they looked manlier than dress shoes or sandals, and not to associate with "sissies."

Larry White was a drum major in the band. He'd pretend to come and see my sisters, but all the time he was trying to see me. So this went on until my senior year of high school. I graduated, got a job at J.P. Stevens Factory cutting tablecloths, and went to community college at the same time. In 1979, I made a choice to leave Roanoke Rapids and move to DC, hoping to find a well-paying job.

Chapter 2

A NEW LIFE IN THE NATION'S CAPITAL

In 1979, Thomas Sweatt moved from North Carolina to Washington, DC. He settled with a friend of his, Floyd Newell, "also a Christian brother," in an apartment building on the corner of Fiftieth Street and East Capitol Street NE (one block from DCFD 30 Engine). *That's where I met my best friend, Floyd Newell, who was also from North Carolina. He passed away in 1988 from AIDS. We did a lot of clubbing together. He had a good job at Woodies (Woodward & Lothrop). So basically, we just worked to buy clothes, look good, and go to the clubs and dance. We loved to frequent bars such as Lost and Found on Half Street SW, Clubhouse at Georgia and Upshur streets in Northwest, and Tracks in Southwest. Those were good times!*

My first job in DC was at Holly Farms. It was located on Nannie Helen Burroughs Avenue NE, which intersects Division Avenue NE. It was in the shopping center that back then had a Safeway. I believe it's a church now. No, I didn't burn churches. Never, ever—that's God's house. I could walk to and from work not knowing the danger late at night. Yes, there were fires back then that I set, but as I grew older the fascination grew stronger. There were some near misses, close calls, and some near-death experiences. But somehow, I managed to survive a long time. One last thought—there was a barber shop off a little road that leads in the same area where I worked at Holly Farms. That was where one of the fires occurred in 2003.

I made the choice to serve the Lord but fell by the wayside. I do believe in God and pray for my forgiveness for my evil deeds. In this place of darkness, one needs some type of spiritual guidance to endure each day God puts before us.

I used to call the DC firehouses to mess with them. I would dial every single firehouse! My fake out would be pretending to be looking for other firefighters. If I called the station and the fireman who answered sounded sexy, I'd continue the conversation to keep hearing his voice. Then I'd hang up. I'd repeat this at other stations. Some would get angry when I talked about nasty sex. That just made me want to call them right back. Different ones would start answering the phones. Even the lieutenant would answer angrily.

I tried the drinking phase to see what it was like. I never got that drunk. I couldn't function. I tried drugs but never got hooked on it. Later in life, I drank socially and smoked cigarettes. But drugs and alcohol were bait to lure young boys for sex. Sorry.

This is where his path of psychological and physical destruction would begin. Mr. Sweatt would "frequent that area (30 Engine) a lot."

I even parked my car in the rear of the fire station to take a nap. I would feel so tired from hanging out and lighting fires at night. Unlike the fire station on Capitol Hill (near the Navy Yard), the gate was closed.

When you and I were talking on the phone, my mind was just wandering of all the residents in that area where there was a fire. Like the Fort Chaplin Complex (in 1982, near the Sixth District Police Station) or that little cute house up the street on Dix Street with the fence (2004). Mr. Riffe, I'll stop here before I get too carried away :).

I really want to see more of the pictures of Engine 30. After all those years of wishing to go inside of a firehouse, at least you allowed *me the opportunity to take a mental tour of what it's like. I used to walk in the alley (or drive into the alley) and peep inside the fire station on the 3200 block of Martin Luther King Avenue SE. I could hear their voices talking loud and laughing. I wanted to be amid their conversation and fantasize.*

From the time Mr. Sweatt moved to Washington, DC, he lived in several different locations and boarded in cheap rooms all over the city for several years before finally settling into an apartment on Lebaum Street SE (where he resided when he was arrested).

While living on Lebaum Street, Tom lived in the same apartment building as a DC firefighter. *When I found out about his schedule at work, I waited for his next shift. He left real early in the morning–about 5 a.m. He had a long trip to the fire station on Connecticut Avenue NW, so he had a good little hump. I went and got the keys to his apartment and knocked first before opening just to make sure he was not inside. I opened the door and called his name. There was no answer, so I walked in. His apartment was junky but not dirty. He had weights set up in his bedroom, which I found attractive, as well as his shoes all over the floor. The most important thing was his firefighter boots, the original ones. I took the boots back down to my apartment and set them on top of the gas stove. I'm not kidding. With one boot on each stove burner, I turned the gas pilot on and slowly the leather started to melt like lava. It smelled good, though. While each boot was burning, I had the camcorder taping it all. I went back up to his apartment and washed the boots off. I did see him wearing them again, but soon they were in the trash. I took them out of the trash and kept them for a while until I got tired of them and threw them away.*

Jon, there were a few times when the law found me. I was shoplifting at Bloomingdale's in Rockville, Maryland. I made one trip too many to get this nice black leather jacket. I made it out the door but didn't make it too far. Those charges were later dropped. I once took a friend's car after staying overnight at his house (Twelfth and N streets NW) and left before he awakened. I was staying in the Logan Circle area with my sister at the time, and she found out after he called. That was dumb because I had already given him my phone number. I can still hear her saying, "Tom, what have you done now!?" It was a misdemeanor. The final charge resulted in no jail time. I was caught driving his car on Benning Road NE, near Stewart Funeral Home.

Most of my employment was pretty much the same. Like I've already mentioned, I had the job at Holly Farm from 1979–1982. After that, I worked at Church's Chicken on Rhode Island Avenue for six months, Roy Rogers at Third and Florida Avenue from 1984–1986, Roy Rogers from 1987–1990—which later became Hardees—at Fourteenth and Rhode Island Avenue, then to another location at Thirteenth and K Streets NW, where I was terminated for being rude to a customer. I worked myself up through the ranks from cook to assistant manager. I could get my own apartment and a car. I sported a Fiero, which was popular in the 90s. I took pride in keeping it well maintained. I got along well with my coworkers. I was honest for the most part. Mr. Thorn and Mr. James were nice general managers.

In 1993 I got the job at KFC located at 1944 Bladensburg Road, NE. Bill (the General Manager), hired me as a cashier, and then to a cook. He was later transferred to KFC East Over Shopping Center in Oxon Hill, MD. I worked under Clinton Polk (General Manager) and later was promoted to Shift Supervisor during several changes of Managers. In 2003 I was promoted to Assistant Manager. In 2004, I received the position of General Manager (in other words the Market Coach) which gave me the store to run.

I received several awards along the way and was well respected because of high standards. I truly wanted the customers to have good quality products and for their meal to be hot and fresh from the start to finish. I had good relations with employees. I worked long hours, sometimes opening and closing the restaurant. I'd open work stations when my employees would call in sick, etc. I worked on their off days or birthdays. But for the market coach to put the entire store in my hands was not a good idea. I was not qualified to take on the responsibility. Could I refuse? No. It was my job. Things became very stressful. I took off work for about two months in November and December just to go home to be with my family. That was the last time I saw Roanoke Rapids, North Carolina.

In the early 80s, probably around 1981 or 1982, I was living on Luzon Avenue. One day, I came upon three teenagers near Georgia Avenue and Crittenden Street NW. I was walking toward them and all of them just burst out laughing at me, especially one, who called me a faggot. He was the tallest and cutest of the three. He was like the perfect candidate to take home and shower with whatever he liked. As I passed them heading home, the devil spoke to me. "Don't let them get away with this, Tom. Go back up there and get them." And the devil won. I did just as he told me to do. I went home, got my knife, and headed back up there. They were still hanging around, playing Pac-Man machines. He turned around and grinned at me—it hurt for real because he was so cute. I just walked up to him and stuck the knife in his stomach. I didn't stick around, and I was gone!

Tom always felt that while living with his sister, they were "close but yet far away."

We didn't discuss our personal lives, be it good or bad. We never talked about our problems, so I really didn't have anyone to talk to. My sister carries part of the blame for where I'm at today and my family will one day tell her because I lived with her for all the years setting fires. She told my family she didn't have a clue and that there weren't any signs. Her take on it is that she thinks I gave up on life and went to jail because things would be easier there. She doesn't think or want to know the other side of Tom.

One time she and I were sitting in the living room of my apartment watching Channel 9 news about the house fire at Bladensburg Road and South Dakota Avenue (the green house by the bank). The lady at the house was telling the news crew that she heard footsteps walking up the porch. It sounded like a big man, she said, because the steps were loud. We looked at each other, shook our heads, and said that was awful and we'd be glad when they caught him.

Another time, she called from work asking if there had been another fire. I told her yes. If she only knew it was her brother who was the serial arsonist. But I kept getting away; I sometimes forgot I was the person myself! We were both coming out the back door and that same night, I was on my way to setting a fire because I had a device (Author's note: The device was a jug of gasoline with a rag) in a backpack. She was just taking out the trash. She would ask to use my car sometimes and a device would be in the back trunk. She smelled gas but thought it was used for the lawn mower. On the back porch, there were old rags, towels, and old socks along with a red and yellow five-gallon gas can. Some of the stuff would be in her face, but then if you don't think about fires, you don't really care.

I torched cars parked in front of our building. Some of the cars were just too sexy for me, like the yellow 2001 Cadillac. But my focus for those cars was to keep the drug dealers from parking on our street. It worked for a while, then I quit. One tenant (name removed), watched in dismay as I set a car on fire. The next day, she spoke to me and said, "I saw you do something very disturbing." Of course, I played it off because I had a hooded jacket on. Her boyfriend still lives in her apartment. He stopped a lot of my recruiter interviews. He would come out of his apartment as the recruiter was coming to the door. I was so mad! The whole neighborhood had gotten hyped to Lebaum Street being the stop for all the military.

Chapter 3

FIRES IGNITING IN METROPOLITAN DC

*E*ach fire I set was different. But the car fires had a common message, which was, "If I can't have it, you can't either!" So I used fire as a tool to have the power to destroy. But when I would see someone driving around in a new car to replace the one I burned, I'd think, "Okay, you can have that one." Watching people scramble out of burning buildings, I felt as if they needed my help, so I would just stay and watch. Driving away from the scene, I would masturbate while thinking about the fire.

My thing with fires is not only the addiction, but also the feeling of being in control. Without the fires, I'm powerless—nothing but a mere existence. I would blame the people who lived in those houses. They made me do those things out of jealousy. I would think, I'll never have a house with a porch like that. Or with the cars, I'd think, They're fancy and new and I will never afford them. Seeing the children, I'll never have them because I like men. Watching the family, I'd think, I live alone without a family. After it was all done, I glorified my work and looked forward to the next fire.

After every fire, on my way home, my mind would be thinking about that fire and where the next one will be. I was also thinking, I'm feeling lonely. I need to see somebody. I need to talk to someone who needs help. I want to help to make myself feel worthy and better. I'm finally at home. I opened the car door, parked in the Safeway parking lot at the back of Lebaum Street. It was real dark. I had my apartment key already in hand to open the iron-bar back door. The kitchen light stayed on for security reasons. I was glad to be home. I undressed and got right in the bed. But before doing that, I put a tape in and watched a previous fire or a recruiting interview, masturbated, and fell asleep. If I had trouble sleeping, I'd lay there thinking of so many things; my family, the fires, where will it end, and what will tomorrow bring! I got little sleep. When the next day came, I was ready to face the day! But it was always the thought of setting something on fire. That was daily!

Jon, you asked me to tell you the "details, etc. of every arson, your feelings, etc." To answer would take forever because there are just too many fires. The ATF gang counted nearly 350. So I don't know how you want this part of the list done. Most of them were in Northeast DC, the rest in Maryland and Virginia. And it's not just houses that were burned, but cars, cop cars, Metro buses, places of business, gas stations, car washes, etc. The ATF team has a map of all the fires. Each fire was different and had a special meaning. I loved the smell of fire and burning rubber.

I need to see you so we can really talk about this stuff. The expressions on your face will let me know that you understand what I'm trying to say; just as Scott, Tom, and Bob (Arson Task Force) did. I'm sure you'll be eager to listen. Did I say listen? That looks like a foreign word! I didn't get too much of that in the real world. Yes, I had hobbies growing up. But for the past twenty years or so, setting fires had become a hobby (sad to say) or a pastime! Some people like to play sports, listen to music, go fishing and hunting, or just go to the movies. I spent my spare time seeking out and planning fires, whether driving around DC or on a long trip to Virginia or North Carolina. There were some successful times and not so successful times. Like a drug addict, I had to keep the flames burning! It's a feeling of being relieved.

Most of the fires were taped, and I would go back to watch them on TV. I would write the date and location so that when I wanted a specific one, it would be labeled. The same with interviews of armed forces recruiters who came to my apartment looking for the imposter nephew :)! That was a lot of fun, but also a very long story. I have some regrets about being too shy to really take advantage of what was right in my presence. We'll discuss that later.

The ATF recorded it about right—there were at least 350 fires. As the years passed, the car fires outnumbered the house fires. At some point, I was burning one car (or more) a day. It had become so much fun to watch it slowly burn, then explode—especially the US government ones and also SUVs. I tried to burn every last one of the US government vehicles at the recruiter's station in Silver Spring, Maryland. Just as you go under the overhead path, it's on the left and the fire station is across the street. This was the recruiter's station new location after I burned them out from their old address, which was just a block away. At the old address, I drove up to the back of the building and parked. It was about 6 p.m., and they had all left. I could smell the office odor from the tile on the floor. The frosted-like window of the bathroom was slightly cracked. I opened it some more and started finding paper and stuff to throw on the floor. There was a trash can nearby, so I got whatever I could out of there. I lit a match and watched it slowly burn. I called the station the next day and the phones were dead. I knew the fire was a success, and I was happy for that.

Around 1980–1982, I lived on Luzon Avenue, and I used to wander around in the Petworth area near New Hampshire Avenue and Georgia Avenue. While living there, my friend would walk the street to get picked up, and guys would take him home to have sex for money. I was young, just twenty-seven years old. I only wanted to just look good and have sex. The neighbors did not like it and told my sister they were going to sign a petition to evict me. Thanks to her, she offered me to come and live with her at the Iowa, located at Thirteenth and O streets NW. The neighbor that told my sister that drove a black 190-class Mercedes. So my sister let me use her burgundy 1969 Camaro to move my stuff.

After I was out of there, my mind started having these thoughts of "Oh, hell no. They aren't going to get rid of me that easy!" So I thought about the lady's black car. "Go burn it up, Tom." I drove by and splashed a quart of gasoline across the front windshield. I drove back around the second time, pulled side by side, stopped, lit a match, and threw it across the windshield causing it go whoosh! Sometimes I would ride the bus with a quart of gasoline in a backpack. As years passed, I started carrying a briefcase that was full of dangerous stuff like a salad knife (from Roy Rogers) and a pocket knife that I found. I was into flatting tires a lot, and that pocket knife came in handy. I got a kick out of hearing the air leaving the tires or walking outside the next morning and seeing one, two, three, or all tires flat.

Sometimes, I used to sneak into empty Metro buses and tear the seats out to use the cushions to burn the bus. That never worked too well because the fire didn't last long before burning itself out.

There was a charter school next door to KFC on Bladensburg Road where I worked. I set fire to so many cars in our parking lot. It wasn't so much that the cars were taking up space for our customers, but the fact that some young student was driving a certain car. I chose his car because I either liked him, what he left inside the car, or just the car itself. Some of the fires, I taped myself doing it. I'd place the camera on the ground of the parking lot. It was funny watching me be sneaky and getting in and out of the car with a KFC uniform on.

I used to drive through Riverdale, Maryland, a lot after work. There was a fire in Seat Pleasant, Maryland. I remember driving on a two-lane street, which had a wire fence separating it from the highway. It wasn't Suitland Parkway. I kept driving, looking and wondering which house I wanted that night. I came up on this newly built two-level home set far off the road between two other houses. It was a light purple-rose kind of color with aluminum siding. It had a circular window, through which I could see the stairs leading up to the second floor. On the front porch was two pairs of black Adidas tennis shoes, which I took back to my car. I also noticed a red and yellow child's toy and a burgundy Camaro-looking car parked in the driveway. I knew or figured a young couple had to live there. I liked that. I wanted to see if that was true.

So my heart was beating real fast now because I'd made up my mind to set this house on fire. I placed the jug inside the storm door, lit a match to the rags, and watched it slowly burn. I drove past a couple of times to see the flames rushing up to the top part of the porch, and the fire was getting higher and higher. I knew it was going to do damage. I love watching the flames and smoke. "Mission accomplished," I thought. I drove away hoping to get away without the police stopping me. It was hard to remain calm doing something like this because what I'd just done was set somebody's house on fire. What are they doing? What are they saying? The following morning, Channel 4 News with Jim Vance was talking about this address.

I used to remember every single fire years ago, but as time passes, they are slowly fading out of my memory. I can picture the names and location. I only did a few house fires in the daytime. Fort Chaplin Duplex off East Capitol Street SE (near MPD Sixth Precinct) was one of them. Yes, there are a few that linger in my mind because people were killed. Like Mrs. Lou Edna Jones on Evarts Street NE, Mrs. Annie Brown on Montello Avenue NE (it wasn't her house but the neighboring one), Ray Picot and his wife at First and Florida Avenue NW, and the man who the EMS brought out on a stretcher with a little baby. He was burned. All he had on was his underwear. I'm not sure if he survived, but I know the baby did. Jon, this was the apartment building near Engine 3 on P Street NW. I used my sister's burgundy Camaro that night. I went searching, and I chose this building because it was set off from the street. I believe it's the only apartment building right in that section.

I went inside the unlocked door and walked down the steps to the lower ground level. There was a pair of construction boots at the apartment door on the right as I walked down the steps. That's what caught my attention—to set that one on fire. First, I took the boots outside and put them in my car. I came back with a long towel and placed it at the bottom of the door because it had maybe a half-inch gap. I poured the gas slowly so that it would seep inside more than outside. I stepped away, went up the stairs, and lit a match. I threw it at the apartment door. The towel kept the fire from exploding real loud, but it blew me on out of there. It just takes your breath each time, but I had to do that to feel relieved of so many things.

Then I'd see coverage of the fire on TV the next morning and record it. Back then, a lot of fires were being blamed on drug addicts, etc. They did not know that all that time it was the work of arson. I'm sure there were many unsolved fires that I had a hand in but were never investigated, mainly because so many were in black, poor neighborhoods, like Southeast DC.

When you said you worked at Engine 26, it reminded me of several fires in that area. The barber shop at Twelfth and Monroe, car fires at the Brookland Metro station, a house fire on Tenth Street near that bridge headed into Edgewood, and an apartment building (under renovations along with attached houses). I'll tell you about that in one minute. Another car fire, though, was at a residence near Providence Hospital. I followed this person off South Dakota Avenue until he reached home. When he cut the light out in the upstairs bedroom, I knew he had gone to bed. The house I just talked about on Tenth Street was a big fire. I rode through that neighborhood that early morning (around 2 or 3 a.m.) looking at the houses and which one was the safest to set fire to without getting caught. It was a row house with a back porch up top instead of on the ground, so I had to walk up some steps to get to it. I set the jug of gasoline with a sock at the kitchen door. I struck a match and lit the sock. I left and when I came back around, the entire porch was burning, the smoke was billowing and I could smell it.

The next day it was on the news, and they said the arsonist had struck again. In 2004, the same area near the bridge, there was an apartment building and that had a huge fire. Ask the firefighters at Engine 26 and they'll tell you about all these fires because their station is the closest. It amazed me, because from Twelfth Street I could still hear it burning. This fire burned two or three houses that were attached to the apartment building. I liked that fire because the entire building was just engulfed in fast-burning flames.

I almost got caught one night when I was walking around in my neighborhood. The neighborhood had an idea someone was going around setting houses on fire. At that time, I didn't have a car. I wanted to do this house because there wasn't nothing in there but drug addicts. But for this particular house fire, I just had some old newspapers and a little sixteen-ounce bottle of gas. So on this particular night, I crossed MLK Avenue, walked pass the PEPCO building at MLK Avenue and Seventh Street, walked halfway through the block, cut through the alley, and went through their backyard to the porch. The porch had no brick foundation, so I could crawl underneath. That's what I did, and as soon as I lit the stuff under the porch, a small white car stopped real quiet. I looked up, and he jumped out of his car from the alley and said, "Hey, you! Yeah, it's you who's been setting these houses on fire." I started running toward Popeye's, crossing the street, and he came after me. He was trying to get other people's attention to stop me, too. I ran as fast as I could and he did, too, but the only thing that saved me was I hid underneath a porch that wasn't closed in. I lost him. But he was close by because I could hear him asking, "Did they see..." I'd get over it, though, and start thinking about the next fire.

One fire I promised to tell you about was at 4920 North Capitol Street NW. It's a red brick apartment building. In the back, it had flights of stairs to enter each unit with screen doors, which were attractive. There was a basement apartment in the back, too, but it had iron bars keeping someone from coming down the steps. The kitchen light was on. Now this is 3 or 4 a.m. The alley was wide and paved, which made it a little easier to keep the neighbors from hearing *the wheels of the car. I finally decided this was the building for the night. I parked on North Capitol Street a block away. I got out of the car but not before grabbing the black plastic bag setting in the back seat (which contained the gallon jug of gasoline and a sock or cloth tied to the handle of the jug). I closed the car door and walked toward the apartment building. With nerves a wreck, I paced back and forth through the alley until I felt the coast was clear. The next move was to go up the steps to the apartment and sit. I then pushed backward on the porch to the screen door, which was unlocked. I set the device inside the screen door and waited a few minutes to think.* Does the door open to the kitchen? If so, this will be a huge fire because that's where all the appliances are. *I'd made up my mind to do it. Most of the time, I'd say to myself,* "I'm sorry, but I need his fire right here." *I'd strike a match and light the sock. It would start to slowly burn, which gave me time to walk away swiftly before it reached the jug to explode. All that happened, but the tenant who lived in that basement apartment saved the building and perhaps lives. He used a garden hose (which I already saw hanging against the rails) to douse the flames before the fire department came. So the building suffered mostly smoke damage on the outside and inside some of the units. The building was boarded up, so it may have been worse. Oh well, just have to wait for the next time. I was a little frustrated at him for interfering :).*

My mind is drifting toward Southeast DC over on Milwaukee Place and Martin Luther King Avenue. It's a real short street and just a block from Lebaum Street. Saint Elizabeth Hospital is across the street. A charter school sits in the place of the old Safeway store along with trailer courts in the parking lot of the McDonald's. It's been six years, so it could be different now. But during the 90s, there was a fire at the Boys and Girls Club in the back of Milwaukee Place, which has old, run-down (some condemned) houses lining the street. There is also a football field with bleachers on one side. The maintenance was poor— the grass grew tall and had a lot of weeds that grew out into the alley, which made it difficult to drive through the narrow space. I squeezed through a hole in the fence to get to the field and walked to the gym. There were steps that led to the back. I could see inside the gym. The floors looked like concrete or tile. I saw the basketball courts, etc. "But will it burn?" I asked myself. It was worth a try anyway. The door was metal. But back there in the dark, in the secluded area, it felt good. I knew nobody could see me. I placed a bath towel at the bottom of the door and poured gasoline through the crack so that it would seep inside. I lit a match and watched it burn. The flames reached the top of the door. I walked away and went to the apartment. I stayed outside on the porch for a while. I could see the smoke, and the smell was stimulating.

On Sunday mornings, a group of guys in the neighborhood would get together for a game of pick-up basketball. I could sit on my porch and watch them play. They would pull in the parking lot with their cars—some had old model cars, some had pretty cars with hot-rod looking bodies with the big tires and rims. One by one, they parked until the parking lot was full. It was very risky because not all of them got out of their cars to play basketball. Then some would forget something and come back to their cars. I just waited to choose the car that I wanted to burn. When the coast was clear, I would open the door and put a lot of newspaper under the dashboard. I would light a match and watch the inside fill with smoke. Then the vehicle would start to burn. The owners would come running to watch, but by that time, the car was on fire. It was satisfying to hear them say, "Damn, damn!" Then they would look around to see if they saw someone who did it. I would be on the porch looking right at them.

Chapter 4

DEATH OF MAMA LOU JONES

On June 5, 2003, at 4:30 a.m., DC Fire and EMS received a 911 call about a house on fire at 2800 Evarts Street NE with a report of an elderly lady trapped inside. Firefighters arrived on the scene and found heavy fire emitting from the residence. They located a fourteen-year-old and twenty-four-year-old in the front yard who had jumped from the second floor. Both advised that an eighty-two-year-old was trapped upstairs in a bedroom. The grandson attempted to get out of the house, but the smoke drove him back.

Firefighters entered the house and found their grandmother unconscious but breathing. Medical crews initiated advanced life support interventions and CPR and transported the grandmother to MedStar.

Shortly thereafter, she was pronounced dead from smoke inhalation and burns. "At this point," said Frank Molino, a veteran detective of the Metropolitan Police Department Arson and Explosives Task Force, "the investigation took a whole new turn. When you are dealing with an investigation with a fatality, there are different challenges than a regular homicide investigation because you're dealing with a scene where basically everything is burned up. You are dealing with a scene that is a lot more chaotic." The fire appeared to have originated in a porch area. There was heavy fire damage to the front porch and front door. "We deployed an accelerant K-9 protection dog who was alerted to an unknown ignitable liquid on the front porch," said Molino. "We ruled out any possible sources of electrical heat or a gasoline container that may have been on the porch. We had to rule all those things out, everything was ruled out. We determined the fire was caused by arson."

Mr. Molino started investigating this incident as a possible homicide. He learned the victim, Lou Edna Jones, was a well-loved resident of the close-knit neighborhood. Everybody called her Mama Lou. "If she had a cook-out, if you was walking down the street, you'd say, 'Hi, Mama Lou.' She'd tell you, 'The gate is open.' That meant come in, even a stranger."

"Why would somebody want to murder and set the house on fire of an eighty-two-year-old grandmother?" Molino asked. "So we looked at other leads, grandchildren of Ms. Edna Jones, were there any disagreements or arguments?"

I loved seeing others take pride in their landscaping and admired Mrs. Lou Edna Jones' yard. It had a pretty bed of roses and pots of flowers leading to and going up the porch. Sitting on the porch the night of the fire was truly a nervous moment. I felt comfortable sitting in her swing and the indoor-outdoor carpet was neatly installed. It looked new. The house lit up like a Christmas tree when it caught fire. I could hear the fire popping while driving back around to watch it burn. The flames were a light yellowish color. I'll always remember Mrs. Lou Edna Jones' house the most. It was the most publicized. Had I not seen her tall grandson leaning out the front door to get the mail out of the box, her house might have been spared.

During the same hour of this fire, I had also set a house on fire at Fourteenth and East Capitol Street SE. Perhaps that's where most of the fire personnel was and because of that, the Evarts Street fire didn't get help in time.

Chapter 5

DEATH OF BESSIE MAE DUNCAN AND ROY PICOTT

*H*ey, Jon! Come ride with me back down memory lane as I take a mental trip to Florida Avenue NW. You can find this location easily. It's near the intersection of First and Florida Avenue NW, maybe the third or fourth house. If you're driving from the KFC going west on Florida and North Capitol, the house will be on the right.

This house is on the list of fires. It happened in the 80s, maybe 1986 or 1987. (Author's note: The fire occurred on January 11, 1985, on Quincy Place NW.) It was a tan brick row house. I'm quite sure it's been remodeled by now. I had worked the evening shift at Roy Rogers (now a Burger King) on Florida Avenue (just as you pass under the path crossing New York Avenue). There's a subway there now, too. I remember exactly what I was wearing a chocolate brown leather jacket, white dress pants, a striped Perry Ellis shirt, some Bally's sandals, and carrying a burgundy suitcase. I didn't like wearing uniforms home from work. At that time, I lived in the Logan Circle area. So from work to home, it was about a thirty- to forty-five-minute walk. It was during the winter because snow was on the ground.

I closed shop and headed home. As I was walking toward North Capitol Street, crossing the intersection, I came upon a man walking the opposite direction. We nodded our heads as to speak to each other. I looked back and saw him pat his pockets as to see where his house keys were. Then he turned to the right to go up the steps where he lived. My mind started to wander. Go back, I thought. Go back to see which house he went in. I did and saw him put the key in the iron-bar gate at the bottom. The iron-bar gate was probably their security. He was light skinned, medium height, wearing a stocking cap, jacket, blue jeans (Levi's), and tennis shoes in the snow!

I got home, changed clothes, got the car keys, and quickly drove back to the area. I took with me a bath towel, a gas container, and matches. I drove back and forth thinking, Do it! Do it! I wanted to see him again and watch him ask for help. I parked the car on First Street and sat there to make sure nobody was walking around. I got out, walked toward the house, and up the steps with the bath towel and thirty-two-ounce jug of gasoline. I pushed it under the door and the iron gate. The door seemed old; it was probably the original door to the house and had never been replaced. I knew it would likely burn fast. I checked for traffic left and right. The coast was clear. I lit a match and threw it under the door. I could tell there was fire inside because the smoke was coming from under the door. I quickly walked back to the car and sat to catch my breath.

I breathed a sigh of relief—I did it! I must have driven past that house up and down Florida Avenue about five minutes before the fire trucks came. I saw him standing outside on the porch in a T-shirt and underwear. The feeling of loneliness and sadness started to go away. I could reach out to him and ask if he needed help. Roy Picott told the Washington Post, "I woke up and fire was all around the bed." His wife, Bessie Mae Duncan died. I did keep the article, too.

Sweatt later wrote that he went to the funeral for Bessie Mae Duncan. For unknown reasons (he never explained why), he never went inside. He stood outside in the rain alone.

Chapter 6

NATION'S CAPITAL CONTINUES TO BURN

There was a fire at 2804 Thirtieth Street NE, in 2005. It's the next street over from Evarts Street NE. If you're traveling eastbound, the house sits right on the corner of South Dakota Ave NE. At that time, the porch was trimmed in white with railings, a white door, and a burgundy awning over the front window. The house was narrow and had a driveway. Two old model cars were parked in the driveway and another was parked on the grass. It had a nice size backyard with picnic tables, etc. It looked like a real comfortable place to just hang out and have some family or friends over. The late model cars attracted my attention—perhaps a son or a husband lived there. I liked the house, too, because of its structure, and it also had an upstairs.

One day, I happened to drive passed it and saw a young dude sitting in the chair on the front porch. That put the icing on the cake. In my mind, I got to thinking, "Yeah, I'll be back tonight."

Sometimes I did roam the neighborhood looking for prospects because I could see better what the house looked like in the daytime. The feeling is like when people go looking for that dream house to buy. Instead, I would be looking for that one house to burn. The same thing with Mrs. Lou Edna Jones—her nephew had leaned out the front door to get mail out of the mailbox. I saw him as I drove passed. When the TV news reporters from Channel 7 came to her house (after the fire), I saw Pat Collins and Gary Reals.

I returned to the house on Thirtieth Street about 1 or 2 a.m. I parked on the other side of the street directly in front of the house. It had some steps around the side to walk up the porch, which led to a narrow door, like a door to the dining room or bedroom, I couldn't tell. The room had three long windows with blinds. I walked around a while checking out the backyard, which was fenced in. I wanted to go back there but was afraid a dog might be there. The parked cars were driving me crazy, too. I wanted to burn all three of them, but my mind was set on the house.

After getting up the nerve, I went back to the car to get the device. I walked back across the street to the house, set the device by the side door, lit the rag (which was tied to the handle of the jug), and waited a few seconds to see if it burned before quickly walking away back to the car. I got in the car, drove to the intersection of Thirtieth and South Dakota Avenue, turned right, came to the stoplight, turned right on Bladensburg Road, and circled back around to find the side of the house engulfed in flames. I must have said something like "got him"—meaning the house was on fire. The fire was growing fast and the flames had started to reach the roof. I circled around one more time, and I could see the smoke and flames from the next street. I was driving faster and crazier because I wanted to get that last look before the fire department started to come. I lowered my car window down to smell the smoke—I loved that part of the fire. I could hear the crackling sound of the fire. I had seen enough, it was time to go. I took South Dakota Avenue toward home, thinking about that fire and wondering what's going on. No one was hurt, but once again a little old lady lived there.

I did not realize that some of the victims had come to KFC with vouchers from the Red Cross for food, etc. I asked one lady what happened, and she said her house had caught on fire. That same house was the one I set on fire the previous night. She did not know that the man who did that was taking her order. And the same for Mrs. Lou Edna Jones' grandson. One day, I saw that he was a passenger siting in a red van in the drive-thru window. I took the money for the food and told them thank you and have a nice day. I recognized him at the house.

Another night, I was on the prowl looking for a house to burn. It was on a Saturday morning around 3 a.m. I hadn't left too long from KFC when I came across the Sousa Bridge on Pennsylvania Avenue SE, and I turned right on Minnesota Avenue SE. As I kept driving, there were two cute houses (back then, one was painted gray and the other one was red brick). I had always admired those houses. But those houses weren't what I was looking for. I made a turn onto some street near them (don't know the name). I parked my car in the alley in a little two-space area. It's a neighborhood full of nothing but two-story row houses with backyards, trees, grass, old junk cars, piles of stuff, etc. So I got out of the car and started to just browse around looking at this house and that house, thinking which one would be the best to burn. I couldn't start the fire at the front because they're all brick houses. I needed some wood or screen doors to start the fire. Once again, I stayed too long looking and peeping down basement doors. I had on the very same uniform that I was wearing the day I was arrested for the arsons.—a blue long-sleeve KFC shirt, black pants, and black KFC shoes.

Little did I know this man was watching me the whole time. He came out of his front door, walked around the side of the house and into the alley with a little gun. It looked like a .45 caliber at the most! I was scared, but I couldn't let him know it. He approached me as I pretended that I had lost my watch, looking down on the ground for it, and he said, "What are you doing in my backyard?" I wanted to run but then he probably would have shot me for real. So I cooperated when he said to start walking and I did! I kept my hands on my head, but I was really scared. I pleaded several times in a very feminine voice not to shoot me. I figured if I spoke softly, he would think, "Oh, that ain't nothing but a faggot, let the fag go." We must have walked from out of his yard, through the alley, and into the street until he just let me go. I ran so fast and so hard when he turned to go back. Then as I found my way back to the car, I heard all these police sirens. Some I passed leaving the area. But he made me so mad. So the next day, I drove past his house and threw a brick in the front window!

There was a fire at Amherst Avenue in Wheaton, Maryland in 2005. It was during the winter months, and I had to take one of my employees home from work at KFC. He had closed that night. James was real young, about nineteen or twenty years old, and a very good cook. All the employees liked him, and his original recipe chicken tasted sooooo good! I dreaded the trip because driving from DC to Wheaton, Maryland, was a good little hump. I felt like it was my duty to see that my employees got home safely. Of course, I stayed equipped and ready with the device in the trunk just in case I got the urge to set something ablaze. I had already put that in my head before we left the KFC parking lot.

I passed plenty of houses and apartment buildings along the way—looking left, looking right, and stopping and slowing down. I was saying stuff like, "Yeah, that's a good one right there." I may want to come back for a house because of the way it's styled or the car or SUV parked in the driveway. I would set the car on fire and not the house, or both. I'd say stuff like, "Wonder what the back looks like."

The Amherst Avenue fire was in a complex of cute little condos with patios. Really comfortable looking. I would have liked to live there. By now I had dropped off James farther up the street from where the fire was. I kept driving through the neighborhood until I found a spot. It was in a location where nobody could see much of the front. There was a motorcycle parked on the patio. That was attractive. Could there be a son, brother, husband, or boyfriend living there?! That was the motivating factor. I started to get aroused. But I had not built up the nerve to do it yet. I sat in the car a long time making sure no more people would drive in from work, etc. Everybody should be asleep! I always kept the keys in the ignition so as to be ready to take off as soon as the device was lit. Okay, I'm ready, I thought, with my hands a little shaky. I got out of the car, walked to the house, and placed the jug at the patio door. I struck a match to the sock and walked back to the car, which was just right in front of it. I started the car and slowly drove away but circled back to see if it burned. You could see the smoke through the complex. I watched the news that morning and learned it did a lot of damage to several units. Some had been boarded up and windows broken out. That was my payment for driving all the way to Wheaton, Maryland. Ha ha ha!

I would frequently give rides home to coworkers at night. Some lived as far out as Mount Rainer, Maryland, Silver Spring, Maryland, or Lanham, Maryland. Yes, I scoped their neighbors while driving to and away from their residences.

There was a fire in Riverdale, Maryland, in an apartment complex where I took the cook home one night. That's the only incident that happened with one of my employees. He thought he was all that, and I wanted to prove that he wasn't all that. I don't think anybody was injured because the apartments had balconies. I knew he lived in the basement level because when I'd give rides, I'd always wait to pull away until they (my employees) were inside the building. So I set the device at the bottom of the steps and lit a match. I drove away and came back around to find the hallway full of fire and smoke. A passing fire truck blinked its high beams. I blinked my high beams. They waved, and I waved. I breathed a sigh of relief.

There was a fire on Alabama Avenue SE in the middle of MLK Avenue and Wheeler Road SE. The Courtland Manor Apartments are across the street. There's also a little shopping center nearby with a liquor store. This area used to be nothing but projects for many years. Then the HUD demolished them and built town houses. I kinda liked them when the construction work was underway. I would drive through there and park the car. I'd get out and walk to the property through the gate and go behind the town houses, looking and peeping, trying to find the one I'd like to live in. I came across this town house that had no door yet. So I jumped up to get inside only to find that the interior was only a frame with wood dividing this room from that one. I recognized the bathroom with the water pipes, etc. I looked around the first floor, feeling comfortable as I looked out the front window. I walked upstairs and came back down to see the steps that led to the basement, too. All my life, I've lived in somebody else's basement apartment! So I made up my mind this would be the house. It was getting dark, too, so that was good. I was thinking this was going to be a big fire (and that the gas line would erupt and burn down all the other units). I walked around in the house with my arms folded, getting the nerve to strike. "All right, let's do it," I said. It was dark now. I went back to the car to get the 7-Eleven bag with the jug and cloth and walked back to that empty shell. People were out but not in view across the street. I wasn't really thinking that the fumes in the air could cause a quick reaction if I lit a match and threw it on the gasoline. I might not have made it out had I not been at the top of the stairs in the basement. This time, I poured the gasoline on the bathroom floor and went along the edges of the rooms. The gas smell was really strong, and I had walked in it. I went to the top of the stairs, struck a match, and within a second it went WHOOSH and BOOM. The quick flames caught the hairs on my arm, eyebrows, and a little of my hair on fire. That was scary and I kept saying, "That was close, that was close." I made it outside, got in the car, and just sat there for a while to see what would happen. Smoke kept billowing out of the chimney and the air became cloudy looking. I was glad for that. At least all my efforts weren't in vain. It burned all night long, and the next day the fire department had boarded three or four units. I loved the smell of smoke. The only thing missing was the people running out of the houses yelling for help. I would have come to ask, "Is everything all right? Can I help?"

I had worn out my welcome by calling the army recruiting station in Waldorf, Maryland. They wouldn't send nobody out to see me. So I came to the army recruiting station one night. When the police were cruising through the parking lot, I was leaving and I asked him directions to get back to DC! I was in the middle of setting a US government car on fire, and the officer showed up. But when he left, I did what I set out to do, and that was burn that pretty, sexy army joint up. It was a pretty orange-colored flame with a lot of smoke shooting up *in the air...*

I followed a 5.0 Ford Mustang around for almost a year before I finally burned it. The owner of that car was always clever. I found it parked in the right spot one morning before going to work at KFC. He had backed it up against the side of the liquor store, so nobody could see me. I could park my car two car lengths beside the Mustang, and I backed my car up, too. He'd always park in view of the street, so I couldn't hide. A white 5.0 Ford Mustang with black interior and tinted windows was truly tempting. I wanted to sit in there and ride with him and watch his foot work the clutch. The sound of the motor running was truly simulating. I liked to masturbate while thinking about a hot rod like his. I set the device at the left front tire and lit a match. I drove out of the parking lot after ducking down to get back into my car. I drove past a couple of times up and down the road to find a female bus driver blocking the driveway. She was on her cell phone calling 911. That was my signal to keep going down South Dakota Avenue and head on home. But from South Dakota Avenue, I could see two sets of flames, so the fire from the Mustang must have ignited the car next to it. That was good to see.

There was also a house fire in Alexandria, Virginia, on Richmond Highway near a shopping center where the recruiting station is. There was also a dry cleaner on the opposite side. The house was way back at the end of the block. It was a real cute little house with a porch on the front that would come up the side. I liked the celery-green aluminum siding. Here I am in Alexandria, Virginia, I thought, so I need to light a house on fire while I'm out here. The fire burned up the front.

Farther up Richmond Highway, there was also an apartment building fire. I did that one during the day time. It was a large complex with speed bumps so that the residents couldn't drive fast through there. It had metal doors though, and I knew there was a possibility that the building might not ignite. It did! With the black bag containing the jug and the cloth, I picked the second-floor apartment where I didn't hear a sound. Perhaps nobody was home. I quietly sat on the steps in the hall near the receptionist office (I could hear her talking) and waited. Oh, I'm ready to do this! I listened for voices and movement one more time up and down the stairs, went to that apartment, set the device at the door, lit the towel, and backed away to my car. I started the car up and just nicely drove away. I decided to just keep driving through the complex until I saw smoke or people. In minutes, I saw a young lady with her child out on the balcony. The smoke had gotten in her apartment. The hall light went out, and it looked really dark inside. It was a nice effort for being so far away from home.

Another time out in Alexandria, Virginia, I found an abandoned service station sitting on the left-hand side (if you're driving south) on Richmond Highway. It was probably the year 2000, and it was an early Sunday morning. The station was off by itself, on an angle, and had bushes and old junk in the rear. I parked along the side where there were two windows with screens and boarded up with wood. It may have been a Phillips 66 from the looks of it. The pumps were old, too. I really wanted to see if there would be a big explosion, given that it was a service station. I was curious to find out anyway, so I had made up my mind that this would be the fire for the night. I didn't have anything ready, no device or anything, so I had to drive to the nearby convenience store to get some stuff. I bought a jug of juice, emptied it out, and set it in the trunk near the gas tank. I may have bought two or three dollars' worth of gas. While standing at the pump I pretended to be pumping gas in the car, but actually the gas was filling the jug, which set right at the pump. The trunk hood was slightly up, but not all the way. I went back to the boarded-up screen windows (with no glass), took the jug, and poured all the gas down the side of the window slowly so that most of the gas seeped inside. When that was done, I paused because the smell of gas was strong. I didn't want to get blown up! The following morning, when I turned on the news, news anchorwoman Susan Kidd was on the scene. I never showed this fire to the ATF crew.

There was a car fire in Maryland near the Eastover Shopping Center. I used to ride the A8 bus (marked Livingston Road). I'd get off at Southern Avenue and South Capitol Street to go to the mall. So if you're driving that route, keep straight past the shopping center until you come to Audrey Lane, and make a left. Go up the hilly street (with the speed bumps) to a huge apartment complex. There are some houses, too.

The apartment front doors were unlocked, which I liked. Cars were parked in the garage, too. I drove around looking and thinking, I like that truck. I admired the color and the custom-made front or grille. It would burn nicely. Then I'd park and hopefully wait to see someone come home. So it must have been 4 or 5 a.m. on the weekend. I wanted this truck. I popped open the trunk and got the jug of gasoline in a 7-Eleven bag with a sock. I set it in the front seat. Now I had to make sure that all was clear and nothing was moving. I was always thinking somebody was peeping out the window. I would look at blinds, curtains, shades, everything. Then I lowered the car windows down and looked at those big tires! I rubbed my hands all over it. I wanted to smell the rubber treads as I get aroused. I masturbated and talked to the tire as if it was a person. I wanted to make love to it. I stopped. I uttered the words, "Look at those big mayonnaise joints on that truck."

Okay, it was time to go. "Come on," I said. The jug was on the front seat. I grabbed it and set it on top of the tire. There was a wide space between the front fender and rim of the jug. That way, I knew it would burn fast. And it did. I struck a match to the wick and watched it burn slowly. I started the car and drove away. I circled back to find it on fire. I was pleased. The black smoke started to shoot into the air. I came back around to find the entire front on fire. I laughed when I heard a big boom. It was so loud and the zzzzzzzzzz sound really got the fire going. I nervously kept driving passed and was relieved that another fire was complete.

One morning, on account of being nosy, I happened to be a witness to a murder at the gas station on Alabama Avenue and Naylor

Road SE. The police roped me in. In the parking lot were a lot of police cruisers, parking meter trucks, and much more. It was also near the homicide division at the intersection of Branch Avenue and Pennsylvania Avenue SE. The next morning, I drove inside, parked away from the unit division, and set a police cruiser on fire.

This fire from 1997–1998 will be a mental trip to one of the places that just popped into my head. I think it was one of my days off work or just coming home in the early morning hours, driving around and searching for a good hidden spot to burn. I drove down I-295 South and took the Bolling Air Force Base and Malcolm X Avenue exit, made the left, and almost went home. Then that feeling came over me, "Don't go home, go straight. Go find a place to set a fire!" I yielded. Sorry.

I remember all too well driving on Mississippi Avenue SE, heading toward Branch Avenue. When I got on Branch Avenue, I came up on Sam's Car Wash (a popular spot) on the right and up farther on the left is Coral Hills or Cherry Hill apartments. I wanted to burn something at the apartment complex, but it wasn't the right setting. There were too many cars and it had security.

It was thrilling to see young thugs hanging out at the bottom of the hill. I parked behind the skating rink to watch people coming and going. While continuing to drive on Branch Avenue, I came to the stoplight. There was an auto-body shop and other stores in that strip of businesses, but they didn't appeal to me. I thought the body shop looked like it would burn nicely because of the wood frame and door. The parking lot was so that I could drive around to the back. That was perfect. I sat back there as darkness fell. I ate something but don't remember what it was. After eating, I stopped and gazed at the steps leading to the basement. I got out, walked to the basement, and peeped inside. There were a lot of pipes and stuff. I wasn't too thrilled about that because it might not burn like I want it to. But I drove all the way there and had to make it count. I felt like a strong man with automotive skills who knew about cars. That was a turn on. I needed to let them know that *the arsonist had paid them a visit through fire.*

I set the device at the metal-frame back door, lit a match, and watched it slowly burn. I got back in the car and slowly drove off. I parked across the street to see the black smoke rising above the roof. I knew the fire was burning. I drove back out there the next day to find the shop boarded up. I was glad for that. The same kind of fire happened at the fabric shop on Silver Hill Road off Suitland Parkway. I think it's the south exit. It's past the Metro Center and a laundromat. That was a good fire too because the back had a screen door with a wood frame. The draperies were attractive in the window as well as the fabric. Sometimes I get mad and shout, "Please go home! Please let me do this! I need to do it in a hurry!"

There were several house fires and car fires in Oxon Hill, Maryland. Some were off Saint Barnabas Road, like if you're going to the Home Depot. There was this one neighborhood with cute little houses and neat yards (probably belonging to families). I would drive from Lebaum Street to MLK. I'd keep going until I came to Alabama Avenue and make a right turn onto Wheeler Road. I'd take Wheeler Road all the way out to Maryland, passing nice homes, before ending up at an apartment complex where there was eventually a car fire. But they locked the parking lot after that fire.

Other times I'd drive past Eastover Shopping Center to Audrey Lane, go to the stoplight, and make a left on Livingston Road. There's a McDonald's on your right. I kept driving until I came to Birchwood Drive and turned on that street. I can't remember the streets the fires were on, though. They were house fires. The first fire was a one-story house. It had pale green aluminum siding. But I still hadn't decided if I wanted that house, so I drove through the neighborhood looking and stopping and thinking about all kinds of stuff. It's the perfect house but wrong location. They might see me. If the lights are out, that's a sign they might be asleep. *It takes time to build my nerves to burn a house.* Will the person inside get out or be trapped? What will he be wearing? *If they're asleep, then no cars should come through to disrupt the fire and call 911. I want the fire to burn a long time—to destroy the house with big balls of fire and dark smoke. After driving through, I came back to the first house after all. It also had a side porch with steps. Trees were on the side, too. I parked near the house on the opposite side. I got out of the car and walked slowly to the house, up the steps, and sat, putting the device at the door. I lit the match and watched the cloth slowly burn, driving away only to return to find the steps and the door on fire. I was the only car driving around in that neighborhood. I came back around to see the whole door just burning. The flames were moving so fast I knew it had to have gotten inside. The last time I drove past, all the lights were on in the house with a man standing in the front yard. He tried to move his car from the driveway, but the car was too close to the house. After most fires, I'd say something like "Got 'em" or "Mission accomplished."*

There was a yellow-colored house that had the cutest screened-in porch. I wanted to go inside and feel the comfort. This house sustained little damage. I was just playing around. There was a car fire, too. I drove out there and parked at the recreation center to watch the young guys play basketball. I saw this man working on his car. I told him (in my mind), "I'll be back to get that car," *and I was. It was a burgundy Chevrolet. Most of the time, I'd go over there in the daytime to just watch who lives where and what kind of car they drove. One dude was walking on Livingston Road headed back toward the McDonald's I referenced earlier. I followed him with the camera, recording him all the way to the Audrey Lane apartments. He wore faded jeans, a white T-shirt, and tennis shoes. I couldn't resist him. He was perfect. He went to the apartment, and I parked in front of it, waiting for him to come back out. He never did. That night I went there to set a fire in that same building, but the door was locked. He was the one that got away.*

I frequented an office building in Landover, Maryland, where there was a marine recruiting station. Jon, I set so many government cars on fire in that parking lot and attempted to burn the office building down. During the day, I'd go out there to hang out. I went inside the building, took the stairwells to the third floor, and opened the door to the hall. I walked slowly passed the recruiter's office. I saw him sitting at his desk. It was a beautiful sight. The windows were decorated with marine stuff, which I adore. Then I walked passed again, and he saw me. The same as the fake interviews—I asked him if my nephew came by and he replied no. But little did he know I had the camera in a leather bag with a cut-out piece for the lens. The sound of his husky voice was too much. I said thanks and left because I didn't want to get caught.

There must have been five or six car fires at the Landover office. At one of them, I came back the next morning after the fire. The car was owned by a marine. I took a pair of pants, a shirt, and a cap out of the back seat of a red SUV that were hanging up. They were the marine pants later found in Virginia (Author's note: Pants are described later. Tom left them at a building fire in Virginia so investigators would assume a marine was the arsonist.) I wore that uniform around in the house with a pair of new, shiny black boots I had ordered from the catalog. It felt good, looking in the mirror and seeing a marine. I'd try to walk differently to look more masculine, but it didn't work. I was still a sissy.

One night I drove way out to Chantilly, Virginia, to see what the marine station looked like. It was inside the Sully Place Shopping Center. There must have been four or five cars (US government). I saw a van and I parked beside it. People were still at work, and it was nearing closing hours. I waited until the parking lot was empty. There was a security guard that kept making his rounds. I'd duck down in my seat so he couldn't see me. The recruiting office sat in the middle of the shopping center, so it was too obvious. But I had to do something to have come this far. I picked the van. I reached for the device and set it in the front seat of my car. I made sure the coast was clear and set it under the front fender inside of the tire. I lit a match and watched the device slowly burn before driving off. I left the parking lot and headed down the highway. I could see the flames and smoke from afar. That's all I needed to see. I did what I came to do.

Let me tell you about the police cruiser fire in Maryland. It's like when you go past Eastover Shopping Center. Again, take Indian Highway toward Fort Washington, Maryland. Just as you pass the mall and drive about five minutes, there was a brick house (that sat alone with plenty of yard). The house was located on the street that you take leaving Eastover Shopping Center. Anyway, it was early morning hours, 5 or 6 a.m., and I had been out all morning from KFC, just thinking and wandering where I can set a fire. I used to drive wherever my mind led me, and on this night it was to this part of Maryland again.

I was attracted to this big, two-story house in which the police cruiser was parked in the driveway, close to the house. I figured if the car burned, the front part of the house would, too. It's just something about a police car parked at home. Is he married?, I wondered, and all that crazy stuff came to mind. This time, I was not prepared to set this fire.

I went to the Gulf gas station near Eastover and filled the empty jug with a gallon of gas and put it in the trunk. Sometimes I had to keep the trunk of the car up to hide what I was doing. Part of the gas went into the car tank and the rest into the jug. I found a piece of cloth or rag out of the dumpster to use as the wick. After all this getting ready at the Gulf station, I drove back to the house. I passed it a few times before parking way down the road to blend in with the other parked cars. I sat there staring at the cruiser and the house. The cruiser was white with green stripes and another orange-brown color. The tires were wide and had plenty of rubber. I liked that. So after building up the nerve to set this car on fire, I got the device, got out of my car, started walking straight and slow, but kept an eye on the windows and yard. I came up to the house, walked up on the driveway to the cruiser, and squat down so that no one could see. It felt good being that close, but I was still not ready. I rubbed the front tires, looked underneath the front of the car, but I still was not sure if somebody was looking out from the window. It's time now, I thought. I slid the device under the front fender inside the tire. Heart was beating fast, though. I lit a match to the rag to watch it slowly burn. I hurried away down the side road, got into the car, and was relieved I didn't get caught. Now I could relax—the car was burning. As like other times, I got a feeling of "Yes! Yes! Yes! I did it," and was gratified by the sight of a vehicle used by a person of power on fire. The raging orange balls of fire and the dark smoke was truly a sight to see. Other cars driving passed on Indian Head Highway slowed down to watch. They probably dialed 911. I did not wait to see the police officer come out, though that would have made it more exciting—I wonder what he looked like. Was he black or white? Probably white by the style of his house. I drove back home thinking about another fire.

The fire on Dix Street was in a little house with awnings on the front and side. It was a real cozy little house, but it was very good for a fire because it sat off to itself and had aluminum siding. It had a big, long porch that I really liked. It was early in the morning about three or four o'clock. I had come from an all-night shift at KFC. I decided to set this house on fire that night. There was a Jeep parked in the yard. I played around a long time, making test runs, first looking around on the side of the house, then walking back to the car, which was parked slightly in front of the house. I just stared at the house wondering who was inside and if they were asleep.

All this time, cars were driving past, and I was still sitting in the car. Then it hit me. "Go ahead, Tom, and do it. It's getting late." I looked down the road to see if a car was coming, got out, and walked with the device to the side of the porch. I set the device on the side of the porch near the rail. This way, nobody could really see it. So I never went up on the porch. I just reached from the side and lit the jug of gasoline with the cloth as a wick. I stayed a few seconds to make sure it was burning.

The news the next morning showed that little house with its windows all boarded up. There was some man talking about the fire. And just around the corner off that same street was a car fire—a blue Yukon SUV with sporty tires. I had to have it, and I got it. But that one was risky because the SUV was parked by a street lamp shining bright! I didn't care! I think if I were released from prison, I'd still set fires, but not in DC, Virginia, or Maryland. I would have to start in a fresh area or city, preferably in the South.

Did I ever tell you about the barber shop fire at Twelfth and Monroe streets NE, just a couple of stores down from the sub shop? When I was living on Quincy Street, that's where I used to get my hair cut, and I only wanted the barber, Mike, to cut my hair. I enjoyed him touching my face and neck, and his body kept rubbing up against my back and shoulder while he cut. I eventually lit the barber shop on fire. Why? Because Mike didn't care about cutting my hair like he used to, and I didn't like that.

Evarts Street NE, Channing Street NE, and South Dakota Avenue NE were just a few streets where fires happened. There was a little house with green shingles right there at the corner of Bladensburg Road and South Dakota Avenue. The lady's hand was burned, and I remember her saying she heard big footsteps coming up the steps. That fire was a desperate one because I had been working all night and was tired. But when that feeling hits me, any old place will do. She (like Mrs. Lou Edna Jones) had a neat yard with pretty flowers. It was never my intention to hurt elder people, but that was definitely the case. The front door was engulfed in flames when she tried to open the door. I liked her porches, too.

On February 5, 2002, members of the District of Columbia Fire Department were called to 1210 Montello Avenue NE, Washington, DC, for a reported fire. A subsequent cause-and-origin investigation revealed that the fire was intentionally set (with an incendiary device) by the pouring of an accelerant. It was further determined that the smoke from the fire spread through the walls to the adjoining house where eighty-nine-year-old Annie Brown resided. Ms. Brown suffered from smoke inhalation and was taken to the hospital where she died on February 14, 2002. Ms. Brown's remains were transported to the District of Columbia Medical Examiner's Office where an autopsy was performed. The autopsy revealed that the cause of death was smoke inhalation and the manner of death was a homicide. (Author's note: A search of Mr. Sweatt's residence on April 27, 2005, revealed a newspaper clipping about the fire.)

One fire that never leaves my mind is of course the fatal fire on Evarts Street NE. The fire was started by using a gas-soaked towel lined at the bottom of the back door. I knew there was also a dog inside. What made that fire so big was it touched one of the gas pipes and burst into flames. But this fire burned a long time before the fire trucks arrived. And the firehouse was only two blocks away! How pitiful is that? The black smoke billowing up in the air was a beautiful sight, and the smell was getting me all worked up. It was so dark; the streets were closed.

Where I lived, the yard was so well maintained. I cut the grass, trimmed the hedges neatly, placed mulch around the shrubbery, and did the edging. Afterward, it felt good and relaxing to sit on the front or back porch. I did a fire at a P Street NW apartment building in 1986 or 1987. That's what drew me to the other residents. I wanted to feel the comfort *and* care *on some of my victim's porches. It could be the smallest house, but if the yard is well maintained, that helps the house so much. Some of the porches, I sat on as long as forty-five minutes to an hour, looking and listening to any type of noise that might cause distraction or make me lose concentration to carry out the mission. I'd take several deep breaths, pondering over and over, Do it! Then the same thought: Do it! But things didn't always go as planned. The fire wouldn't start, etc. So I'd have to park and go back up on that same porch and finish lighting the sock tied to the gallon jug of gasoline. It's definitely a relief to drive back around the corner to see the house engulfed in flames.*

A two-story white house sat on a back street near Silver Hill Road. This was the perfect target for an early morning sunrise fire. I had been riding all night searching for the right house, but I kept going back and forth thinking, "No, that's not it." So I chose this house because the front door had no screen. I could easily set the device right at the door and the fire would creep inside. The family was displaced for a year or so, but it was remodeled after. The fire just basically smoked the house up.

There were car fires at the Fox Hole Apartments that were never reported. It was good to go back to the area the next day to see the car burned out. And also during the daytime on my off days from work, I would like to hang out at the Marine Barracks at the Navy Yard at Eight and M streets SE. They had a parking garage right under the bridge, and I would go inside (because there was no guard). A lot of cars burned there! But one day, I was getting gas at that Exxon (or BP) station in that area. A white man followed me out of the station all the way to Pennsylvania Ave SE, but before crossing the Sousa Bridge, he stopped the chase. That was close, and my heart was beating really fast. I ran a red light and he didn't. I guess that's what saved me.

During the day at the fire station, also around Capitol Hill on Eighth Street and Pennsylvania Ave SE (Author's note: Engine 18 and Truck 7), I set a fire to their cars as well. They must have been asleep because the cars burned a very long time. Watching my fires was like having a good cup of hot coffee to help you wake up in the morning. "I'm ready to do it again!"

There was another fire at East Capitol Dwellings apartment complex. This one took a lot of nerve because I was inside the screened-in back porch at the kitchen door. I knew people were home because I could see the light from the TV.

I didn't do many vacant properties except the development off Alabama Avenue SE and the Southview Apartments on Southern Avenue (on the Maryland side). The Southview Apartments were just across the street on the Maryland side and were newly developed *and still under construction. It started to rain that morning. The* Washington Post *reported the damage to be close to $1 million. The fire ruptured a gas line, and that's what I had intended to do. The flames were so high that they were reaching across to the occupied units. It was a huge fire, and I kept driving up and down Southern Avenue (between Wheeler Road and Galveston Place near the Post Office) thinking,* "Wow, what a fire that is." *The big orange flames were just beautiful. I parked to watch. A loud pop sounded off as a lady and I were stopped at the red light facing the opposite direction. I could hear her saying,* "Oh my God, good gracious." *I stared at her with the look of* "Why is she up this early in the morning?" *I could hear the fire truck sirens getting closer, so I knew it was time to leave.*

Some of the fires, I'd say stuff like, "Here I am, come get me," *or* "Look at them," *(meaning the firetrucks or police),* "They don't know I'm right here!" *I'd drive up and down the street to watch until the streets were blocked off. One fire, the firetrucks and police cars were right behind me. I knew I was gone that time, because I had just set the barbershop on fire at Nannie Helen Burroughs Avenue NE.*

I can still hear the boom boom *from the music being played as I walked into the apartment building (near the Marlow Heights Shopping Center), where I set the device in front of the apartment door. It was on the second floor. He was able to jump out the window but broke his leg. Again, I must have sat in the hallway about thirty minutes getting the nerve to strike. I also liked Wheeler Road. There were lots of good projects there, and cars. It was the ghetto and I loved it.*

I used to call it "surveying the land." *Things I would often ask myself were, will it burn quickly? Is it aluminum or wood siding? I hoped the family or resident would come out (but not get killed). I wanted to see them scramble for safety, and then the fantasy would kick in. I wanted to come back and help a son or boyfriend who might be injured. I could ask,* "What happened? Are you all right?" *But it was a good feeling knowing I just set a house on fire and got away. I always want* each fire to burn a long time before the fire department arrived. There's the white smoke when the fire was extinguished. At the same time I felt sad for the victim but would say, "I had to have that house, or that car, or that building." Then I would start planning for my next fire...

I took advantage of the winter months because it was cold, nobody was out, the windows were closed, and there was less chance of people hearing footsteps, etc. When driving around in the wee hours in the morning, nothing was moving, and it seemed like I was the only person out on the road. I felt alone and sad, and that contributed to lighting a house, a car, or a building. My motto then was "Me against the world."

I never told anyone about the fires. Yes, I knew there was a $100,000 reward. And I saw when they posted fliers of the forensic sketch of me. The photo was placed in gas stations, 7-Elevens, etc. in Maryland and DC. That was a good picture, but it looked more like my father at a young age. I was right across the street all the time and would walk in the gas station and fill my jugs up with gas. The description was correct (a black man with salt-and-pepper hair). That was it.

Chapter 7

MEN IN UNIFORM

O*kay, Mr. Riffe, I have to admit (without going any further), that I have this fantasy of men in uniform. Oops! Did I mess up?! Please say no. But for real though, it's true. It could be firefighters, police, Metro bus operators, military, etc. That's why I asked for pictures of firehouses and fire trucks because the images of fire trucks racing off to fires or other emergencies drives me crazy! I want to be right there amid it all, soak in the smell of the fire, watch the fire itself billowing into the air, see the water hoses and the urgency of the crew. So I guess life is just one big fantasy. Sometimes when I would get off work, I would drive by military recruiter stations. I would film them from my car and later masturbate to the videos :).*

The military recruiters were always coming by. (Author's note: Tom would call the military recruiters and tell them that his nephew, who was fictional, wanted them to come by because he was interested in joining the military.) *The camera would be hidden in the closet to tape the interview, with the closet door open just a crack. But as time passed, I became braver and set the camera right on the floor where we were. They saw it sometimes but didn't say anything. I would rearrange the furniture to have them face a certain position in front of the camera. It was mainly to capture the angle of their lower body, legs, thighs, and feet. If I liked their face, I'd zoom in to tape only the face while the recruiter was talking. If two recruiters* came at one time, I'd say, "Sorry, he's not here, can I take a message?" I didn't do twos. If the recruiter wasn't attractive, I'd not let him in, either. Mean, right? At the end of the interview, they'd leave. But as the recruiter walked to get in his car, I'd come to the front door and signal him to come back and say my nephew is on the phone that's in the bedroom, still with the camera running. He'd return and walk with me from the living room to the bedroom and answer the phone. Of course, nobody was on the line. That was my chance to close the bedroom door and try him. See whether he'd fight or push me away. Either way, it would have been gratifying to my soul! The sound of him getting away was stimulating. Trust me...if I had those days back over again, some of the recruiters would not have gotten away too easy!

There were recruiters who came as far as Newport News, Virginia, and Richmond, Virginia. One sergeant drove his government car from Newport News to my apartment. There's plenty of military in that area because it's near Naval Station Norfolk. It was about 8 p.m. when the recruiter from Newport News knocked on the front door of Lebaum Street. I almost missed him, but I happened to look out the living room window and saw him getting back in his car. I signaled for him to come back and he did. He asked for Jermaine Bryant (the fake nephew I made up), and I told him that he had gone up to the corner store and would be right back. "Please come inside and wait," I said. He did. He was about six foot two, light skinned, and weighed about 215 pounds. He was a perfect candidate. So we talked a long time while sitting in the living room. He sat on the sofa, and I sat in the chair. The camera was taping our conversation from the bedroom. It was positioned at the door to get a view. I was nervous and smoking cigarettes one after the other. He was really a hunk of a man. Feeling tired and fatigued from the long drive, he dozed off. I lit a cigarette and put it on his black shiny shoes to smell the leather. It burned a few seconds before he awakened. I played like I had dropped the cigarette. He asked, where was Jermaine? Did he get cold feet? But while he was talking, his legs and thighs were opening and closing real fast. That made me more nervous, and crazy thoughts were coming inside my head. I should knock him out with something and have sex with him, a MARINE! *Would I get away with it? I didn't know. I didn't do it because I was having too much fun having recruiters keep coming to my house. It was late at night. He was just that close to being my company for the rest of the night, and who knows the rest.*

Of course, there was never an interview, and I played like I was tired and had to get up early in the morning for work. I went into the bedroom and left him alone. From the bedroom, I could still see him sitting on the sofa. When he fell asleep again, I went and stole his cap (white with black leather strap and eagle symbol). I hid it in my bedroom closet. He woke up and started looking for it. He even opened the closet door, walked lightly to the dining room, and peeped into the bathroom. I recorded all that. His walk was perfect. I watched it all on TV and kept rewinding and pausing, rewinding and pausing, especially when he was walking back to the dining room. Then he just opened the front door and left. That tape was never recorded over. When the ATF confiscated the tapes, that scene was still on there. Jon, there were dozens of recruiters that came by my apartment. There were some stories about them too that will make you think, "No, Tom. You didn't do that!" (Author's note: Many of the recruiter's names have been omitted to protect their identity). *This was another hobby (besides setting fires). I love it, miss it, and think of those military guys every day.*

When I got tired of using the Lebaum Street address for recruiters, I had them come to Mellon Street SE. I would be fixing up a vacant unit. That's where I met another sergeant around noon one day. He was a body builder. I was not expecting him! My heart skipped a beat. I put my tools down, went to the front door, and pretended Mike (my fake nephew) had just walked up the street. The recruiter parked his car under the shady tree, and I went to talk to him again. He was eating a Snickers candy bar. I saw his beautiful, black shiny shoes and his blue dress pants with the red stripe looked neat on his thighs. He was real friendly, and I wanted to get inside and talk with him. He waited about fifteen minutes, then walked back to the building. His shoe strings were dangling over his size twelve shoes. I recorded his feet only to and from his government-issued car. I couldn't wait to get home to watch it on tape.

He would travel back and forth again several times to pick up "Mike" to take him back to the recruiter's station. His final trip to Lebaum Street was when he called to speak to Mike, and I pretended to be Mike. I changed my voice to sound more masculine and like a teenager. It worked.

"Okay, I'm on my way," he said. "You're not going to stand me up, are you?"

"Naw, man," I said in a very manly voice.

He came. I was nervous. I set the camera on the dining room table in a leather bag, but I cut a hole so that only the lens would show. He walked in the front door to the apartment, and I asked him if he would like to come inside and wait. He said yes. I pointed where I wanted him to sit so that the camera would be directly on him. He didn't feel comfortable because he kept looking around. I went to the bedroom after the phone rang. When I answered the phone, it was another recruiter looking for Mike. I said he wasn't there and took a message. Now, the sergeant was still in the living room alone. While still in the bedroom, I was thinking, what should I do? This will be his last trip anyway. I wanted to get him angry and fight me just to record all his sounds, the voice, the stomping of his feet, and of course his body movement. I decided to play it off that and told him that Mike's been playing games all along and to just leave. He stood up, and I said "leave" while walking him to the door. I went to touch his shoulder. He raised his arm and stiff-handed me. I liked that! As he got to the door, I opened it and spanked his firm, tight butt. He felt solid (just like a piece of beef)—real solid. He didn't know what to think of that, but he turned around and walk out the door. I ran to get the camera to see him walk the long way to his US government car. I must have watched that tape about 100 times!

Chapter 8

HOMOSEXUAL LIFESTYLE

*J*on, I never had sex with a female. People don't believe it, but it's true. The closest I came to a girl was when this chick came from New York to North Carolina to visit. I kissed her. It didn't feel good, but I felt it was the right thing to do. My first sexual experience with a guy was when I was a junior in high school. It was near my house on the field where we played baseball. After the games were over, people started to leave. We were the last two to leave, and he had a bike. He asked me to hop on up front and he sat on the bicycle seat. When I looked back at him, he had his penis out. It was large and I saw the head. I didn't say anything, but I liked what I saw. We both got off the bike and went into the bushes nearby. We laid down on a broken-down fence. We kissed and his tongue was down my throat. It tasted musky, but I liked it. He told me I should have been a girl because I was pretty. We kept kissing, and he pulled my pants down and started to feel my behind. He asked to fuck me. I said no, not this time. He said, "All right, I'll be back." He never did. I was glad. Little to learn that he soon enlisted in the service as a marine. How cool is that? I kissed the lips of a military man. He died about two years ago. I wished I had a picture of him.

At the present, I don't have a significant other. I had one intimate relationship in the real world—that was during the 90s. His name was Tyronne. His mother lived in the Fort Chaplin Complex (which is also on the list of fires). He was an amateur boxer who stayed with his aunt

(Auntie Alice) on Third and Peabody streets NW. A friend had let me keep his car while he worked an evening shift at the US Post Office. So I went out cruising up Georgia Avenue NW after midnight. He was walking up toward Kennedy Street NW, and I stopped to ask him if he needed a lift home. He nodded his head, or should I say he shook his head and said no. Feeling rejected, I persuaded him by repeatedly asking, "You sure, you sure?" When he turned right toward Kennedy Street, I made a right turn, too. He could see I was determined, gave in, and got in the car.

My heart was beating fast, but I couldn't let him know I was nervous. He only lived a few blocks away. I asked could we keep in touch. I gave him my number to call. I doubted I'd ever see or hear from him again. Lo and behold, he called the next day. I was happy. I lived at Fourteenth and Luzon streets NW, so he was in walking distance for real.

Our relationship consisted of getting drunk, smoking "reefa" (weed), and watching TV. His favorite show was Dynasty. He would come over most Wednesdays and we would watch it together. Sometimes he would stay overnight if he got too high and fell asleep. He was really good at telling jokes and playing backgammon.

I wanted to have sex, but he made me wait weeks :)! He was attracted to me and vice versa. But what caught my eye when he was walking up Georgia Avenue NW was his tennis shoes—"chucks" or Converse (white and blue, size thirteen)—football jersey, and blue jeans. As a child, big shoes always aroused me. I always liked to masturbate over my uncle's and dad's shoes and sleep with them in my bed.

I lived in a nice neighborhood but had no business there because I couldn't afford it. I worked at Roy Rogers (which is now a CVS). I loved Tyronne and wanted to be number one in his book, but he told me I could never be number one, only number two. I had a problem with that. I bought him new clothes, new tennis shoes, etc., to keep him. I supported his wants and needs until I went over his aunt's house one night. I saw him leave with a girl. He lived in the basement, and he left the door unlocked. I opened the door (and left the door open for light), gathered up some of his clothes and shoes, put them in a suitcase, and took them back home with me.

His aunt's house was on the corner and also on the list on fires. He called the following morning to say that someone had set Aunt Alice's house on fire. It sounded funny, his voice was low. I pretended to care... He never knew what caused the fire and eventually moved to South Carolina. I saw him later in the 1990s sitting at a bus stop on Pennsylvania Avenue where a KFC stands at the intersection. I chose not to bother him.

While living on Quincy Street, I bought a white 1987 Pontiac Fiero. It was a two-seater but very sleek, and I had a high-top fade haircut and a jet-black beard. I was too busy cruising, picking up guys, and going to BASS Liquor Store on Rhode Island Avenue in Mount Rainier, Maryland. I'd buy coolers and drink Hennessey and use cocaine. We'd go back to my crib and drink, watch TV, and have sex. Sex for me was cuddling up, touching, caressing, and kissing, which most guys don't do. That made it more exciting for me. When they'd fall asleep, I'd move quietly out of the bed. I'd pick their shoes up and smell them. I'd wait until the guy was really out of it and snoring. I'd move his legs so that I could get close enough to kiss his penis, kiss his lips, and smell the alcohol on his breath. I would stand away from the bed and masturbate while he was sleeping.

One of my hobbies was to ride the Metro bus (preferably in the early morning hours when there's nobody on the bus), looking for good-looking drivers who wore black patent leather shoes. I'd pay the fare with the transfer ticket to ride to the end of the line and pretend I missed my stop. Usually the driver would let me ride back down without putting extra change in the box. I'd sit behind him and place the hidden camera under his seat and record his feet working the pedals. The glitter of the shiny shoes excited me as well as the sound of the brakes, then the acceleration—what an awesome thrill! It was truly worth the hours of waiting and wandering. I made so many tapes of just bus drivers.

One night I picked up this dude on Bladensburg Road NE at the bus stop. I took him to wherever he was going, and he told me he had been in the marine corps. That's all I wanted to hear. I told him I would pay him for a kiss! He did. I was surprised, but it wasn't that good. His mouth was sour and the tongue didn't feel right!

Sergeant Riffe, you asked me why did men's shoes have such a sexual satisfaction for me. It's hard to explain the feeling. As a child growing up, the feeling was there and is still there now. I don't know. I like to smell shoes. The muscle and the odor are stimulating. It's a man's shoe, and the bigger the better! In an environment where there's nothing but institutional boots and shoes, it's just what the doctor ordered! But the shoe must match the individual's foot, walk, etc. You see, Jon, there are all kinds of feet. There's pigeon toe, slew footed (which means left foot points out to the left and the right foot points out to the right). And please don't be knock kneed. If a man wears the right kind of shoe for his feet, it's sexually satisfying.

Usually the feet are what catches my eye first, whether it's a businessman, athlete, blue-collar worker, or just a regular person. The sex part is in my blood and veins. I have names for them when I'm turned on: cock docks, dud dads, and even mayonnaise joints. As a child, I used to hump my Uncle Howard's shoes when he was away from the house. Then at night time, I'd go around to the side of his house to the bedroom window and masturbate while he walked around in the room. I would do the same to my father. I'd go to his bedroom window and peep through the shades or blinds while he was lying on the bed reading the paper. He wore slacks and even while he would have church services in our home in the living room, I would get aroused just by looking at how he was sitting with his legs wide open, and the black dress shoes on his feet were truly divine! There was a church brother that lived in Oxford, North Carolina. He wore these orange-tan color shoes that drove me crazy. One Sunday, he and a couple of other church friends were standing in the back yard near the porch. I went in the bathroom where I could see him, and I would just masturbate over and over looking at those shoes. Another time was at his father-in-law's carpark where I sat side by side and put my feet against his shoe to touch it. This lasted for about thirty minutes. Today, I fantasize over him at his house in Oxford and having sex in the basement.

During the 1980s, I frequented clubs like the Lust and Found, Tracks, The Washington Square, The Delta, The Room, and The Clubhouse. I did have one-night stands. It was mostly kissing and rubbing our penises together. I thought that was enough. Little did I know that it was more to sex than just that! But no matter how many times I had sex or with whom, there was this void that would never go away. The feeling of loneliness and depression would never go away. I'd end up going right back to the same club, hoping to find that one person who I wanted to be my lover, and all the other stuff that comes with it. I didn't realize I was looking in all the wrong places—cruising up and down Georgia Avenue NW, all the way across town, looking for a man! That was crazy! I still do that in prison. I like to watch guys workout as they are doing right now. The bare chest, boxers, and shorts are something to behold. But I try not to let them see me lusting after them. I'll put a cover over the window and look through the peeping hole of the door and masturbate. That way I can see them, but they can't see me. It's truly a good feeling!

The mere fact that I got pictures of a DC firefighter is truly divine :). I put them down and find myself looking and staring at them repeatedly. Jon, this is good stuff. Thank you soooooo much. I'm forever in debt to you. I love all the photos, but I must say my favorites (a) you in your Class A Uniform (b) you standing in front a burned-down house.

You look as nice as you sound on the phone and in casual wear as well. You brought me back to life :)! Your hair, I like it. This happened during the cold months. On my list of fires were also several barbershops. They fascinated me because there were always attractive men in there.

You had on a wool cap (which I like), a heavy sweater (DCFD), and the walkie-talkie. Did this happen in the District? This is what I look for when reappearing upon fires. What the firemen are wearing, from their helmets (and hats and caps), all the way down to their boots, shoes, etc. That's crazy sexy stuff.

I'd ride the 70 bus marked Brightwood (which is the next street after you pass the Gibson Building next to the Fourth Precinct Police Station). The driver made a right turn after emptying the bus and parked on the next street, which is nothing but a field and trees. Jon, I'm sorry, but you're the only person who knows this crazy stuff I did. If I liked the driver, I'd sit behind him and pretend I missed my stop (but really didn't) and pay more fare or he'd let me ride for free. One time, I got the urge to grab the driver's dick while he was sitting with his legs wide open. Well, I did. I got up, leaned over, and felt his dick while he looked away. He said something like, "What are you doing?" I quickly got off the bus, but he chased me across the field before stopping, and I kept going.

Do you remember the Ricki Lake show? She would do shows about hot firefighters. I would go crazy because they would all be so fine and gorgeous. And the Jenny Jones show would do the same thing as well as Bob Barker on the Price is Right. He would do a salute to the men and women of the armed forces. I'd tape them, and you know the rest of the story :). That's good stuff. You might start to think, why is Tom always talking about firemen in uniform? Trust me, Jon, this is the final chapter. I promised. Just remember that a picture is worth a thousand words.

Decades have passed, and those feelings of wanting to have crazy sex is still there. I love being "clear conduct" (Author's note: Clear conduct is the absence of incident reports, violations or "shots") for years, and that's a good thing. I can't mess that up in here. It's like a report card or even a credit card. I can't move ahead without it. But while we are on lockdown, there are inmates who like to stand in the door window to watch TV. If the guy has a handsome, attractive face I like, I'll masturbate to him, but my cell has to be dark, so he can't see me.

Chapter 9

FULL-SPEED MANHUNT FOR ARSONIST

It started to seem that a disturbing pattern of set fires were occurring in and around Washington, DC, around March 2003, as many as eight in the city alone and four in Prince George's County, *Maryland*, which borders Washington, DC, on two sides. Lieutenant Colonel Scott Hoglander of the Prince George's County Fire Department said, "It's pretty strange to have more than one fire in a particular subdivision or neighborhood. And we experienced three fires set to the exterior of homes in this one neighborhood, which generally speaking is a pretty quiet neighborhood. The same time we were seeing fires set in the hallways of apartment buildings, which were not a common practice, but an accelerant was used and they occurred during the same period between midnight and 2 a.m. The fires were usually set near or at an exit door or passageway from the home, their main means of escape, and an accelerant was typically involved with these fires."

Hoglander believed all the fires in his county could be connected and contacted the District of Columbia to find out if similar types of fires were occurring there. Hoglander indicated, "The sheer fact that they were all occurring on the border between PG and DC, I thought it was important to reach out to them." The answer was yes, but the fires occurred on the east of DC along the county line. The fire on Evarts Street NE that killed Lou Edna Jones didn't fall on that grid. Either there was no connection or the suspected serial arsonist had branched out. Whatever was going on, Hoglander believed it was time to coordinate efforts and bring in some added manpower.

Tijuana Klas said, "The arson/explosives group went down to a meeting with him (Hoglander), got the background what he needed help with, was concerned with a series of fires that might be related, but they needed some assistance from our lab specifically and additional manpower as well."

"For them to ask for additional help or assistance, we knew there had to be something to it," said Special Agent Scott Fulkerson. "We knew it wasn't a traditional fire they see every single night in PG County or DC." In late June 2003, special agents Scott Fulkerson, Tom Daley, and Tijuana Klas met with the DC and PG fire and police officials to review case files and decide on a plan of action.

Fulkerson said, "We're looking for somebody who's very dangerous; somebody that can possibly blend into the community, the area, and know the area well enough to get in, set those fires, and get away being undetected and unknown." In addition, the investigators could agree that these fires seemed to be almost, if not exactly, the same:

- *They occurred in the early morning hours between 2 a.m. and 6 a.m.*

- *They were all set at single-family homes*

- *They were set at or near an entrance area or on a porch or deck*

- *They were in similar types of neighborhoods.*

A task force was formed that included the ATF and police and arson investigators from Washington, DC, and Prince George's County. It was agreed that all evidence would be sent to the ATF Fire Research Lab in Beltsville, Maryland. Hoglander said, "Essentially, we were able to collect the evidence then look at it the same day the fire occurred, which was huge."

By early July 2003, the task force was up and running. On June 30, 2003, less than a full week from the formal foundation of the task force, the task force received its first call. At 0357 hours, a fire was set at 2505 Randolph Street in DC. It was ignited near the door. All the pieces of the device were found at the scene.

Hours are expanded to include a graveyard shift from 12 a.m. to 6 a.m. Investigators begin looking into several of the fires. But the evidence collected from the two recent fires in Prince George's County (one in District Heights and the other in Capitol Heights) provided a potential method of operation for the serial arsonist.

Hoglander said, "I remember getting the phone call from my investigators that were working the scene saying, 'we've discovered the jug on the front porch.'" Raymond Kuk, a forensic chemist with the ATF, reviewed both cases. Kuk determined through the gas chromatography mass spectrometer (an instrument that separates out liquid components and provides chemical information on them) that the liquid used to ignite both fires was gasoline.

The next step involved analyzing the melted debris. When Kuk flipped it over, he found a pristine specimen. Kuk said, "Most people, when they pour something like gasoline or charcoal lighter fluid on the floor, suspect that if they start a fire, the entire thing will be consumed. However, it's not the actual liquid that burns; it's the vapors above the liquid that burns." Kuk also found a thin substance that appeared to have come from a plastic bag that had melted onto a hard piece of polyethylene that looked like a container of some sort. They were seeing the bottom of a gallon-size jug, something you would find for water or fruit juice or milk. They also found the remnants of a sock. "So you take the presence of a sock, a plastic container, and this bag together, and you're looking at the various components of an incendiary device."

The evidence began to mount. Analyst Kuk noticed some faint markings on the bottom of the container. "Sometimes there are actually initials or letters or symbols of a particular manufacturer." Kuk examined the evidence from the other home, the one in Capitol Heights, and found the same thing: black and white plastic bags, a charred sock, and a hard piece of polyethylene plastic with similar markings on the bottom. Kuk said, "So at this point, we probably have the same individual(s) doing these things." Detectives did some further digging and found that the plastic jug was a fruit juice container that was purchased at a local convenience store. For investigators, it's like trying to find a needle in a haystack.

"We were able to narrow down and focus on certain stores at least in a close proximity to the fire scenes," Fulkerson said.

"We would actually go in and mark some containers on the bottom with our own markings that we could identify, so if they showed up at the scene, we could trace them back to a particular store, and then in turn look at the surveillance camera inside the store and try and identify who purchased it," Hoglander said.

The trap was set, but Mr. Sweatt didn't play along. Investigators weren't sure if the suspect was onto them or just being cautious. Hoglander said, "In the summer months, it's warm, people have their windows open. The weather is nicer, there are more people on the streets, and it's harder for a person to go undetected."

Meanwhile, investigators focused on what appeared to be some consistent behavioral patterns. Daley said, "We had surmised early on—based on the fact that he was traveling over a large distance and that fact that Metro wasn't running at that time of night—that the individual must have had a car. So we began to try and determine how much time the individual had to exit the vehicle, the time he had to get to the front porch, the time he had to ignite the gasoline, to the time he escaped."

In late summer 2003, investigators gathered at the Fire Research Lab in Maryland to determine how the incendiary device really worked. Tests were conducted on the front of a house built onsite, one that was like the single-family homes set on fire by the arsonist. Kuk said, "the investigators were seeing the burn patterns, smoke patterns, the melting on the vinyl siding, and from that, determined how much gasoline in a jug would produce this type of fire that we're seeing." Results revealed that the incendiary device was designed to create a slow burn. Kuk said, "Typically these things would burn in eighteen to twenty-four minutes, so we're looking at that kind of window or timeframe to place the device, ignite the device, and escape."

The task force then turned to the behavioral science unit (ATF) for help. Fulkerson said, "The typical serial arsonist is a white male in his early thirties and generally a loner. A failure in different aspects of their life might have caused them to reach out and set fires. The person may engage in reckless behavior at work or at home and may lead a secretive life."

As the summer of 2003 winded down, so did the arsonist. Fulkerson said, "It's common for arsonists to stop for a period of time, whether it is because they have something positive going on in their life that wouldn't create stressors that are making them act out and set fire to structures, or they feel as if investigators may be getting close to them."

On September 14, 2003, the case took a strange turn. Three men, brothers and roommates, return to their home on Anacostia Avenue after a night out on the town, only to find a strange man sitting on their front porch. The witnesses in the vehicle said that he simply just came up to the passenger side of the window of the vehicle and said something to the effect of, "Does Mr. Harris live here?" To which the individuals in the car replied, "There is no Mr. Harris living here." And they both went their separate ways.

Upon leaving the vehicle and walking toward their house, they recovered a bag on the front porch. They looked into the bag and saw a one-gallon juice container of Arctic Splash filled with gasoline and a T-shirt. The three men weren't sure of what to make of the stranger or the items in the bag and called the Metropolitan Police Department (MPD) the next morning. The MPD then reached out to the ATF. Detectives canvassed the area while forensic experts processed the scene for evidence. Chemist Raymond Kuk from the ATF was called in. "Immediately we were able to recognize there is a one-gallon container that was left behind with a black bag, that was used in our minds to conceal the device, along with a black T-shirt." The incendiary device was consistent with what Raymond Kuk had seen since the beginning of the case, but that was not all he found. There was a hair recovered on the side of the container. This was the investigators' big break in the case.

All three witnesses told investigators that the man was between the ages of thirty-five and fifty years of age. At that point, they also had a forensic electronic-sketch artist come in and provide them with a sketch based upon the statements that were made in the interview. Investigators know the arsonist's method of operation, and now they had a description of a possible suspect. But they still had no idea who he was or when he would strike again.

Thomas Sweatt described the Anacostia Avenue incident as "the fire that never was." I sat on that front porch too long, looking, waiting, wondering if there was anybody inside. It was a brick house, but the door was wood and I knew it would burn. It also faced the park across the street. Nobody on that side would see. I just sat there too long. The device was in a black plastic bag placed at the door, ready to be lit. The residents (two young guys), drove past at the stop sign and saw me sitting on their porch. I knew something wasn't right, so I got up (leaving the device) and pretended I was waiting for a guy. I asked them if they knew Lawrence Davis. Honest to God, Jon, that's the name I gave. He was my boss at KFC. It was a good name. They replied "naw" in a frustrated tone. I started walking down the sidewalk toward my car, which was parked just a few feet away. They drove around the block and cut through the alley. I ducked down on the hilly grass, and when they passed I got up, ran to my car, and drove away. They are the ones who gave the sketch that you may have seen in gas stations and carry-out restaurants, etc. It was a good sketch, but it looked more like my father. I still went inside the gas stations and didn't think twice about it. I was tired. I didn't care anymore whether they caught me or not. The ATF was getting frustrated. They had a task force out to get me for two years. The same night of the attempted fire, the ATF was parked at the parking lot right beside the Wendy's on Nannie Helen Burroughs Avenue NE. I drove right past them.

At the height of the investigation, fifty-five agents would be working the case at any given time. Mr. Sweatt would walk right past investigators at many points during the manhunt as they were staking out convenience stores. At some fires, investigators were at arm's length away from arresting Mr. Sweatt, who stood oblivious in the crowd of onlookers. Investigators later reviewed video footage of a firetruck responding to a house fire set by

Mr. Sweatt. In the opposite direction was a stopped car, flashing his lights at the oncoming fire trucks. Unknown at the time to investigators, Sweatt sat behind the steering wheel of that vehicle.

Over at the DNA lab, analysts determine the single thread of hair found on Anacostia Avenue belonged to a middle-aged black male, which matched the three witnesses' descriptions. Initially, they were really excited about getting that. Then there was the realization that you really didn't know who the contributor of the hair is. Is it the perpetrator, or is it simply the person who sold him the jug at the convenience store? The hair was run through a database, but there was no hit. That initial wave of euphoria was followed by a more sober moment.

The agents and officers on the task force had more than 100 members during its two-year existence and conducted lengthy surveillance details, day after day, cruising neighborhoods before dawn. Authorities offered a reward for as much as $100,000 for information leading to the arrest of the arsonist. The ATF also developed a profile of the arsonist.

The characteristics of an arsonist included possible alcohol abuse, reckless or unsafe work practices, blaming others for his problems, and frequent lying. How wrong they were. "Arsons are hard to prove," said ATF Agent Scott Fulkerson. "There is limited evidence left behind. Almost everything is consumed in the fire. This arsonist covered three states and multiple jurisdictions. There was a lot of media coverage and great stress to the community. There was pressure felt by the task force to catch this guy. There was an ongoing threat to the community."

The Associated Press reported:

A big reward and hundreds of tips haven't led to the arrest of the arsonist responsible for up to 35 fires around the nation's capital that have killed one person and injured 10. The fires, which began a year ago, have shaken residents in parts of the area that in the past 2 ½ years has seen a terrorist attack, anthrax letters and sniper shootings. "It's a very scary situation," District of Columbia Councilman Vincent Orange stated. Several of the fires have occurred in his ward, and constituents have expressed concerns at community meetings. "I tell them the arsonist has a pattern of doing this between the hours of 2 am and 6 am, and so we need to be vigilant and have a dog or something that can make a noise," Orange said. Since a telephone tip line was established last July, more than 500 calls and e-mails offering information have been received. A sketch of a possible suspect began circulating last month, prompting 150 new tips but no arrests. Profilers say the suspect is likely to be angry or troubled. Studies of serial arsonists have found them to be skilled liars capable of being charming, manipulative and cunning. They also are quick to blame others for problems in their personal or professional lives. "Somebody out there knows this person, and they know that they are out those times of the night or early morning when the fires are occurring," said Victor Stagnero, lead arson investigator for the Prince George's County, MD, Fire and Emergency Medical Services Department. "People are worried, and I understand that. A lot of the folks in the neighborhood are worried that when they go to bed at night that this person might make them a target," said Battalion Chief Gary Palmer of the District of Columbia Fire and Emergency Medical Services Department. Many of the residents' homes that have been damaged are concerned that no arrests have been made. Authorities are advising people to remain alert, keep their porch lights on at night, and consider installing motion-activated lighting on their property. We certainly need people to be vigilant if we're going to catch this guy," Washington Police Chief Charles Ramsey said. Solving an arson is not easy. According to the FBI statistics, only 16 percent of arson investigations end in arrests. Washington-area firefighters have gone door to door in some neighborhoods where the fires have occurred, distributing sketches and urging residents and business owners to be alert for anything suspicious.

Betty Adams, who lives in Washington where seven suspicious fires occurred, said Tuesday she is "frightened to death." "I don't sleep at night much because you never know where he or she is going to strike next," Adams said.

Chapter 10

INVESTIGATORS BEGIN CLOSING IN

During the investigation, a man who lived in an apartment building that has been the scene of three suspicious fires was arrested on a Tuesday and charged with starting one of them. Paul M. Dubois, age fifty-seven, was arrested at his fourth-floor home in the Marina View Towers in Southwest Washington. Officials said he was charged with arson for an early morning blaze on July 23, 2003.

"The whole hallway was drenched in an ignitable liquid. Several containers full of an ignitable liquid were left on the floor," said Alan Etter, spokesman for the District of Columbia Fire and Emergency Medical Services Department. Dubois suffered minor burns in the fire.

"They had no evidence," said Greg Lattimer, Dubois' lawyer. "It's just the fact that the District of Columbia needed to respond to this situation."

Officials were also investigating other fires in the building. On the night of June 26, a flammable liquid was poured on several fifth-floor doors and ignited. Two residents and a firefighter were injured. On July 6, a fourth-floor carpet and door were ignited with a flammable liquid early in the morning, but no one was hurt. On June 27, flammable liquid was poured on the fourth floor, but was never ignited. During the investigation, several fire code violations—including lack of a working smoke alarm—were discovered in the building. The owners were fined $3,000. Meanwhile, investigators were also looking into a series of suspicious fires in the area—fourteen in Washington and ten in Prince George's County, Maryland. "The fire at Marina Towers on which the arrest was based has some similarities" to those twenty-four fires, said Chief Ronald Blackwell of the Prince George's County Fire and Rescue Service in *The Washington Post*. Dubois had not been linked to any of the twenty-four fires or the other incidents in his building.

On October 8, 2003, at 4:14 a.m., members of the District of Columbia Fire Department responded to 1315 Otis Street NE for the report of a fire. A subsequent cause-and-origin investigation revealed that the fire was intentionally set (incendiary) utilizing a suspected destructive device containing an ignitable liquid. At the scene, investigators recovered remains of a plastic jug, a bag, charred fabric material which was adhering to the top of the container, and fire debris. Subsequent investigation revealed that the premises was a rental property and had been so for thirteen years. The tenants at the time had a one-year lease with a monthly rental payment of $1,800. Therefore, as a rental property, the investigation classified the building as used in interstate commerce and in an activity affecting interstate commerce.

On November 16, 2003, at 4:50 a.m., firefighters in Alexandria, Virginia, respond to a building fire at 4410 Braddock Road next to a nursing home. The building was a cottage for the Lynn House, a nursing care facility operated by the Church of Christian Science. The Lynn House leased rooms to nurses who were working in the area longer than three months, and therefore, like the rental property on Otis Street, was a building used in interstate commerce and in an activity affecting interstate commerce.

According to Tom, he wasn't aware it was a nursing home. He thought it was a house. Tom wrote, *"I'm truly glad no one was hurt there. Had I really known that, Jon, I wouldn't have set it on fire. There were no signs in the yard or anything. I liked that house—it was on the end of a road, and there were no houses across from it. I sat on the porch for a while. It had just a little cement porch, just enough for one person to sit. The house was blue. I liked that it appeared that a family lived there. I slowly pushed back off the porch to the door, which was all glass and unlocked. I pushed the door open and set the device between the storm door and the house door."*

Chief Deputy Fire Marshal Bob Luckett was called to the scene. "Units responded and found fire present from the front of the building near the front door." Did the arsonist branch out? If so, he was now all over the map. Tijuana said, "Because of the number of fires we had, the diversity of the victims, we were ruling out the main motives of arson, which are normally revenge or profit. This put this type of arson in a whole new category. It was very hard to figure out what was making it serialized."

Chief Luckett at the time wasn't sure if he was dealing with a serial arsonist, but he was not taking any chances. He called the ATF. "We found the remains of a one-gallon plastic jug and there was an alert for gasoline with it, and of course, again, it was quickly linked to one of our fires." The arsonist has now struck in DC, Maryland, and Virginia. Analysts quickly found that the jug had the same markings on the bottom of the other jugs used at fires. With this discovery, Mr. Luckett was asked to join the investigation.

A look at a dozen other fires in the Washington, DC, area over the previous year revealed more disturbing news. It appeared many of those fires were deliberately set, possibly by the same person. It was logical that this middle-aged man didn't fall from the sky and start setting fires. They began to really look at how long this guy had been doing it, what had he been doing, and what we had missed, if anything.

On December 3, 2003, investigators decided to revisit the Evarts Street NE fire in Washington, DC, that had killed Lou Edna Jones six months earlier. At that time, they had no idea they were dealing with a serial arsonist. Now there was plenty of evidence to suggest a connection. In most of the suspected arson fires, investigators found an oval-shaped imprint of the jug that contained the gasoline. But the Evarts Street fire was so intense that unless the investigators knew to look for the remnants of the incendiary device, it would go undiscovered. "So we took what appeared to be melted carpet, some plastic, and some fire debris and collected it and sent it to the ATF lab for further analysis," said Molino.

"What I was seeing was apparently a melted high-density polyethylene plastic container, and I could see a thin layer of black plastic as well," said Kuk. Kuk confirmed this was the work of the serial arsonist. Investigators now had their first fire-related homicide. If the serial arsonist had killed once, he could kill again. The metropolitan area was gripped with fear, and with no strong leads, the task force braced itself for the next fire.

On Valentine's Day 2004, the arsonist struck again at an apartment complex on Blair Road in Montgomery County, Maryland, just north of DC. Only this time, investigators believed he had murder on his mind. There was a single egress and ingress to the apartment. There was no back door. There was only one set of stairs from the apartments down to the front door of the building. Many of the occupants had to be rescued by the fire department. Outside, Mr. Sweatt watched as an older woman hung from an upper-floor window, gasping for air.

It was a frightening scene, but firefighters were able to extinguish the blaze, and there were no casualties. The primary cause-and-origin investigator's report stated that as the destructive device activated, the burning ignitable liquid flowed across the landing and down the steps toward the first-floor landing. The fire grew up and out, consuming all available combustible materials. The fire burned very intensely, producing high heat and a large volume of smoke and gaseous products of combustion. The fire produced combustions that were untenable, and prevented the occupants of the building from exiting the structure as the fire was in the only stairwell. Occupants were forced to jump from second- and third-story windows, resulting in injuries to some of the occupants.

At the scene, Montgomery County fire investigators recovered remains of a plastic jug, bags, cloth materials, and fire debris between the first and second floors of the building's only stairwells. The evidence was sent to the ATF laboratory for analysis. The requested forensic examinations revealed that the remains were that of a one-gallon spring water plastic jug and a white 7-Eleven plastic bag, which was the same type of incendiary device previously used by the serial arsonist.

There was something more. There was a pair of pants left at the scene. Since the ATF was not equipped to test for DNA, the fabric was sent back to the crime lab in Montgomery County. Analysts swabbed both the inside and outside of the pants to gather as many skin cells as possible. A DNA profile was determined through a method called polymer chain reaction, which essentially copies DNA so it can be effectively analyzed. It was then compared to the DNA samples taken from the hair found outside the home on Anacostia Avenue, and it was a match. The statistical chances that it was the same contributor other than the perpetrator are very negligible, so it was an outstanding day for the task force. Once again, the DNA profile was sent to the FBI database, but again there was no hit. It was another setback to the investigation. "The thing that was difficult was that there really wasn't a pattern we could even figure out," said Tijuana. "Before we would consistently get at least a few fires a month, and then we would go a month without a fire."

In late March 2004, police in Prince George's County, Maryland, got a phone call from school officials. They say a suspicious man claiming to be a fire investigator had asked to see fire evacuation plans for two different schools. Luckett said, "Based upon the description the caller had given, it was a black male and he had a little bit of a white or gray fluff in the front. We had a composite drawing of the individual based upon the description of the three guys on Anacostia Avenue." Were investigators chasing one of their own? It would've certainly explained why the serial arsonist had been so elusive. Then that possibility took on a whole new urgency when a tip led investigators to a resident of the Riverdale Heights section of Prince George's County. Luckett said, "We were able to identify a car that was leaving one of the schools, and then we got a tag and were able to get an address."

A surveillance team was dispatched to the home. Soon after the stake out began, investigators witnessed a man moving boxes out to his car. When they approached him, they actually saw firefighter gear in the trunk of his car. He explained to investigators that he worked for a local Virginia fire department and said his name was Michael Villam. It was uncanny. He looked like the composite that we had. The investigators did some digging to try and connect the dots, while all the while they wonder if all these fires had been the work of an insider.

"You never want to have to call one of your own and ask them the hard questions," said Luckett. It turned out that Michael Villam worked at a local fire department as a hazardous-materials technician. "We got a motor vehicle photo, and we obviously knew what this guy looked like, and we compared those and they weren't the same people."

In early April 2004, investigators arrest the man claiming to be Michael Villam for lying about his identify. Fingerprints revealed his name to be Noel Tyson and he had a long arrest record, including an arrest for the destruction of property. Could Tyson be the arsonist investigators have been looking for all this time? "Now we have him safely tucked away in jail," Luckett said. "This allows us some time to do the things we have to do, and he's not going anywhere." A sample of Tyson's DNA was taken and sent away to the crime lab for testing. While the investigators waited for results, they looked into the suspect's whereabouts on the dates of the fires. Then more bad news: investigators determined that the suspect they have in custody, Mr. Tyson, could not have possibly been their man. Luckett said, "Not only was he not available on these various dates and times, his DNA ruled him out."

On Friday, April 16, 2004, at 3:29 a.m., members of the Prince George's County Fire Department responded to a report of a fire at 2401 Rosecroft Village Circle East, in Oxon Hill, Maryland. A subsequent cause-and-origin investigation revealed that the fire was intentionally set (incendiary) on the exterior of the occupied residence. The residents of the structure (including a mother, a young child, and a grandmother) were asleep at the time of the fire. Evidence recovered from the scene included melted opaque white polyethylene, paper material, leaves, and other debris, including cloth. Forensic examination revealed that the presence of gasoline from the opaque white polyethylene and other debris, consistent with the kind of device previously used by the serial arsonist. Subsequent investigation of the paper revealed that it was a Jackson Hewitt Tax Service advertisement on the rear of a cash register receipt. The advertisement was prepared for the Giant Food Store located at 1414 Eighth Street NW, Washington, DC. (Author's note: Additional investigation revealed that Thomas A. Sweatt made a purchase on Thursday, April 15, 2004, at approximately 1:44 a.m.)

On September 20, 2004, at 4:51 a.m., a fire occurred at 2804 Thirtieth Street NE, Washington, DC. A cause-and-origin investigation was conducted, and it was determined that a fire had been set at the side porch of the residence. An analysis of the evidence recovered from the scene revealed the remnants of a black plastic bag, a white plastic bag, and a one-gallon high density polyethylene plastic jug. Further investigation revealed a charred fabric, consistent with an athletic sock, adhering to the top surface of the melted plastic jug. Again, this evidence was consistent with the type of incendiary device previously used by Mr. Sweatt. Human DNA was isolated from samples found in the athletic sock.

The hunt for the serial arsonist intensified in 2004, but hundreds of tips led investigators down one blind alley after another. Then in December 2004, firefighters responded to a fire in Arlington, Virginia. It was quickly extinguished. Only this time, investigators found something besides the usual trademark jug and plastic bag. This time it appears he may have left a different calling card behind. "Firefighters discovered a pair of green marine pants," Fulkerson said. They were lying out across the street on the curb from where the fire had occurred. The fact that we were across the street from a military base and we were seeing those marine pants certainly led us to begin to think, 'Do we have somebody involved that's part of the military?'" The clothing was submitted to the Montgomery County Crime Lab for DNA testing.

On Tuesday, December 7, 2004, at 5:08 a.m., members of the Prince George's County Fire Department responded to the report of a fire at 4205 Fifty-Third Avenue, Bladensburg, Maryland. A subsequent cause-and-origin investigation revealed that the fire was intentionally set (incendiary). Like the February 14, 2004, fire at the apartment building at the 7700 Blair Road in Silver Spring, Maryland, the fire was set on the lone stairwell of an occupied, walk-up, garden-style apartment complex and blocked the main exit for residents. At the time of the fire, the county arson task force members concluded that the fire was the eighteenth attack in the county by the serial arsonist and the forty-fifth in Washington, DC, Montgomery, Fairfax, and Arlington in the past year and nine months.

The apartment building at 4205 Fifty-Third Avenue includes several rental units and therefore is a building used in interstate commerce and is an activity affecting interstate commerce. Evidence recovered from the scene included the remnants of a melted plastic container, black plastic, fabric, and other debris. The evidence was collected and sent to the ATF laboratory for analysis. The requested forensic examinations revealed the remnants of a one-gallon, high density, polyethylene plastic jug. Gasoline was also detected in the evidence submitted. These components of the incendiary device used in this fire was again consistent with the components of the incendiary device used by the serial arsonist. Also, from the black plastic, white block lettering was visible. The writing read in part "MADE IN CHINA FOR CORNELIUS SHOP."

Additional investigation into this piece of evidence revealed that the bag, in fact, probably read "MADE IN CHINA FOR

CORNELIUS SHOPPING BAGS." Inquiries regarding
the distribution of Cornelius shopping bags revealed that
the company only supplies two locations in the Baltimore/
Washington metropolitan area, including a grocery store near
Martin Luther King Jr. Boulevard and Lebaum Street SE,
Washington, DC, specifically the Circle Seven Convenient
Store. (Author's note: That location is within a block of the
home occupied by Thomas A. Sweatt, which was located at 556
Lebaum Street, in Washington, DC.)

Once again, he left behind a potentially valuable clue.
Investigators could make out a name or two on the plastic bags
left at two of the crime scenes: "Made in China for Cornelius
Shopping Bag Company." Daley said, "The Cornelius Shopping
Bag Company, in Richmond, Virginia, only distributed their
bags to two locations in Washington, DC, and both of those
locations were in the vicinity or close vicinity to many of our
suspected fires."

Investigators devised a plan to stamp each bag distributed by
the Cornelius Shopping Bag Company at both Washington,
DC, stores with an alpha-numeric code on a steel chip. "When
we went to a fire scene to look at this chip," Daley said, "it
would have survived the fire because it was stainless steel.
Then we would be able to look at the date that the chip was
sold at the store and then link it to the video surveillance of
the purchaser." But the serial arsonist threw the investigators
another curve ball. From January 2005 to April 2005, he went
back into hiding. Meanwhile at the lab, forensic investigators
isolated DNA from the waistband from the marine pants. It
was then compared to matching samples taken from two other
crime scenes: the hair found in the bag in Washington, DC, and
the pants found in Montgomery County. On April 1, 2005, the
results come back a match. "The problem is, at the end of the
day, you have no suspect to tie to the profile," Fulkerson said.

Frustrated, investigators contacted the Naval Criminal Investigative Unit (NCIS), which handles criminal investigations for the marines. Fulkerson said, "Our hope was that we could provide them with a DNA profile that we had collected at different scenes and they could query their databases and bring us a matching DNA profile of somebody they currently have in their armed services." The search comes up empty but NCIS investigators mention an open case in their files involving a series of recent car fires around their Marine Barracks. Could this be the serial arsonist authorities have been chasing all this time?

Fulkerson said, "And some similarities were developed from the case files and some other case facts we had. One of their suspects was observed at least in a video leaving one of the fire scenes." The NCIS reviews the video and realizes the suspect car is on camera. From there, it's a quick step from locating the car owner. Fulkerson said, "the address that was associated with that license plate was in close proximity to one of the stores we had surveillance in which the bags were being dispensed." In fact, he lived behind that very store. The suspect's name: Thomas Sweatt.

A background check revealed he was fifty years old, worked at a fast food restaurant, and had no criminal history. Investigators decided to keep an eye on Sweatt. It turns out the restaurant where he worked was in Northeast DC, only a mile away from PG County. Most of the fires were set precisely in those two areas. Fulkerson said, "Not only did he work odd hours, but when he left work, he would drive through quiet neighborhoods, and he would drive different routes every time— enough for us to draw a suspicion to him and more."

Surveillance was conducted outside the residence of 556 Lebaum Street by task force members on April 14, 2005. During that surveillance operation, Thomas Sweatt was observed mowing the front yard of the apartment building and later entering a two-door, 1994 teal Ford Escort, bearing a DC license plate, number CA6649. An inquiry of the District of Columbia Department of Motor Vehicles database revealed that the teal Ford Escort was registered to Patricia Sweatt (the sister of Thomas Sweatt) at 556 Lebaum Street SE, Washington, DC. Investigators followed Sweatt driving the 1994 teal Ford Escort to the Kentucky Fried Chicken/Pizza Hut restaurant on the corner of Bladensburg and New York Avenue NE, Washington, DC.

Intermittent surveillance of the location revealed that the teal Ford Escort was in the rear of the apartment complex in a public parking lot. As noted above, this location was within one block of the Circle Seven Convenient Store, 2713 Martin Luther King Boulevard SE, Washington, DC, which, as mentioned previously, was one of two stores in the Baltimore–Washington, DC metropolitan area with the black Cornelius shopping bags.

On Saturday, April 23, 2005, ATF Special Agent Scott Fulkerson and MPD Detective Frank Molino approached Sweatt at his fast food restaurant where he worked. He agreed to talk. Fulkerson said, "At the end of the interview, we asked Mr. Sweatt if he indeed was the serial arsonist." His response was, "Why would I want to set those homes on fire while I'm trying to be a homeowner myself?" Surprisingly, Sweatt agreed to give a DNA sample right on the spot. Could this finally be the big break detectives have been looking for? It was now a mad dash. Molino and Fulkerson ordered round-the-clock surveillance on Sweatt and rush straight to the crime lab. Task force members observed Thomas Sweatt leave his place of employment at 1 a.m. Sweatt was observed driving the aforementioned 1994 teal Ford Escort to his residence at 556 Lebaum Street SE and parking in the rear of the apartment building. There was no time to waste. Fulkerson said, "So we requested that the DNA be expedited through the weekend."

On Monday, April 25, 2005, the Montgomery County Police Crime Laboratory informed the Task Force that the DNA sample provided by Thomas Sweatt matched the DNA profile for the contributor of the hair follicle from Anacostia Avenue, the piece of pant leg from Blair Road, the piece of sock cuff from Thirtieth Street, and the US Marine Corps dress pants recovered at N. Bryant Street. After two long years, the task force finally knew the identity of the serial arsonist suspected of lighting more than three dozen fires and killing at least one person.

Chapter 11

THE BEGINNING OF THE END

*H*ey, Jon. It's another day the Good Lord has allowed us to breathe; to laugh out loud; sing a song; be happy. Tomorrow is not ours. I feel thankful to be here today. And as always, I'm grateful for our correspondence.

I often think of those athletes in the Gulf who died out in the middle of the ocean in February 2009 (Author's note: Three football players were killed in a boating accident off the coast of Florida). I read that book several times just to learn what happened and how they died. It was only because they were football players, and the thought of them being out there in no man's land, not knowing that death was staring them right in the face, kept me wanting to read more and more. I think about the sharks and other sea life that will feast on their remains. Could a whale have swallowed one of them whole? That excites me because I would love to be that whale...especially if I had the chance to eat Marquis Cooper. What does he taste like? Did he have shoes on? Or any clothes? How long will the whale keep him inside his belly? It's just crazy stuff that only you know, Jon, and that I wouldn't share with others.

Jon, I'll try and answer another one of your questions. You asked, "How did you feel once you knew that law enforcement had evidence you were involved?" It was early in the morning, maybe between 9 and

10 a.m. The arson task force (ATF), Scott, and some black man came to KFC at Bladensburg Road NE when I was at work preparing to open the restaurant. Being the manager on duty, I had keys to the store. I was standing up front, counting the bills in the cashier drawers and in the safe. I heard a tap on the front door. Looking up, I saw a tall white man (Scott) and a black man. I went to open the door, and at the same time, I saw their truck. It was black with tinted windows and was backed up to the door. That's what gave me a clue that it was perhaps some type of law enforcement.

I took a deep breath before opening the door, just to prepare myself for whatever. They came inside and stood by the door. They said, "We're looking for a Sweatt." I said, "That's me, Thomas Sweatt." Scott said my name showed up on their radar. I pretended to be surprised and confused, knowing all along that yeah, they have their man. Scott said, "Could we show you some clothing that perhaps the arsonist left behind?" We went outside, he opened the back of the truck, and picked up a trench coat (like London Fog) and an old hat.

"None of it belongs to me," I said. I was feeling a little relieved.

They asked, "What do you think should happen to this person?"

I said, "That's a terrible thing. He should be locked up and taken off the streets."

Jon, I thought they really believed me, because I didn't fit the profile of a serial arsonist. I maintained poise and displayed polite behavior, even though in the back of my mind, I was thinking, This is it. My time has come, and what do I do now? They told me to have a nice day, and I returned to work. Of course, my day at work was ruined, because now I was thinking they could have arrested me at that moment.

From that day on, the ATF had me under surveillance 24-7. They followed me home from work at night. They told me later after my arrest that I ran stoplights and stop signs! Damn, it's a wonder I didn't get hurt or killed. I kind of felt something was wrong because those little white trucks from the fire department kept swarming around the KFC parking lot and looking inside each day. They staked out at 7-Elevens, especially the one on Bladensburg Road NE near Fort Lincoln Cemetery. That's where I'd buy gallons of juices to use as a device. I'd empty them out and fill them with gasoline.

I never got the chance to do any more fires. I was tired. I didn't really want to be caught, but I knew it would eventually happen. I left a pair of US Marine pants at a fire in Arlington, Virginia. I didn't leave the pants there to get caught; I left them so that the ATF would think it was someone in the military. That was a nice house. It had a pretty yard with a nice fence. The fire did very little damage because I wasn't really sure it if was occupied or not. I didn't set fires to many vacant or unoccupied buildings.

After about two weeks, I thought everything was all right and forgotten. Umm, how wrong I was. On April 27, 2005, I had a managers' meeting at the KFC in Forestville, Maryland, on Marlboro Pike. I got to work and we were all inside getting ready for the meeting—general managers, marketing coaches, etc. Jermaine, the store manager, needed some light bulbs for the walk-in freezer. I volunteered to go. He gave me the money. I left the restaurant, got in my car, but only made it to the exit sign in the parking lot before the black ATF truck pulled in front of me. I was blocked and couldn't go forward. Bob got out of the truck and said, "Put your hands on the steering wheel." He asked for my wallet and keys. I got out and was handcuffed. My coworkers came outside and stared in shock and disbelief. I took a quick glance at all of them because I knew I'd never see them again.

I did not resist, didn't try to fight, and didn't try to run. For what? I knew my time had run out, and the Lord sent them to me before I did more harm to anyone else or even to myself. When you go on a mission, things don't go as planned. I kept silent most of the ride to Greenbelt, Maryland, for the debriefing. They started to take me to Baltimore, but that's if I had of been captured in DC. Thank God, because of all three jurisdictions, DC wanted the death penalty. The debriefing was on the seventh floor, and I'm afraid of heights. So I had to get my nerves up (not to look out the window) to concentrate. I was in what looked like a conference room with a long table. I sat down and looked to see myself on the TV monitor. I was still in my KFC uniform.

It appeared that Scott, the ATF agent, was in charge. He asked if I knew about the fires in DC, Maryland, or Virginia. First I said no to all the questions he asked. But when he said, "We can do this the easy way or the hard way," I broke. Now he was about to start showing photos (about 8 x 10 in.). I recognized the houses (every one of them), and to relive it all over again was not easy. It just started coming back to me: the walking up and sitting on their porches; going around the side and back of the houses, waiting for the moment to strike; the size of the fire and the smell of smoke; all the commotion with fire trucks and police blocking the streets with yellow tape. All that stuff came back clear as day. My family, I thought, how will they be affected? Because they had never suspected any trouble. Scott looked so tired, like he was too glad for it to be over. They gave me KFC for lunch—a two-piece chicken, mashed potatoes, and coleslaw. I haven't had KFC since and probably never will again.

Fire at 2505 Randolph Street NE, Washington, DC.

Fire at 2804 Thirtieth Street NE, Washington, DC.

September 10, 2003: 4713 Dix Street NE,
Washington, DC. (Courtesy of www.dcfd.com)

Rear of 4920 North Capitol Street NW, Washington, DC.

Fire at 202 Quackenbos Street NW, Washington, DC. (Courtesy of www.dcfd.com)

2800 Evarts Street NE, Washington, DC, the site of the fire that killed Mama Lou Jones.

Fire on Otis Street NE, Washington, DC.

Tom (on far left) at a church convention in 1972, Roanoke Rapids. Photo courtesy of Tom Sweatt.

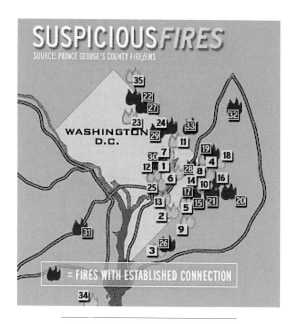

Map of arsons linked to serial arsonist.
(Courtesy of cbsnews.com)

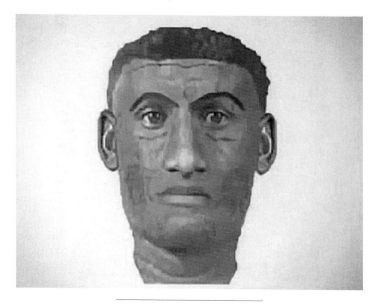

Forensic sketch of arson suspect.
(Courtesy of www.atf.gov)

Reward poster and forensic sketch of arson suspect.
(Courtesy of www.atf.gov)

Hilltop Manor Apartments: 5302 Annapolis Road,
Bladensburg, Maryland.

Location of Tom Sweatt's employment and arrest.

Sweatt, shortly after his arrest, being
escorted to the federal court.
(Courtesy of WRC News 4 TV)

Tom in prison now
(showing off the shoes I
purchased for him).

Chapter 12

ARREST AND CONVICTION

On April 27, 2005, detectives took Sweatt down in the parking lot of the restaurant where he worked.

Luckett said, "We jumped out of the car. I identified myself and advised [Sweatt] to put his hands on the steering wheel, not to move, and that he was under arrest. Shortly after, he was surrounded by twelve investigators." Sweatt was brought into the station house and confronted with DNA evidence from the hair, two pairs of pants, and a sock that tested positive with his DNA evidence, which linked him to the four separate fires. Sweatt played it cool.

"Sweatt didn't believe that we had the DNA until we provided him with some pictures of what we had recovered," Molino said. We presented him with a little more evidence, and finally he confessed and it seemed like, in my opinion, it was somewhat of a relief to him."

Sweatt waived his Miranda rights and gave a videotaped statement to investigators. In that statement, he admitted to being the serial arsonist. He stated that he started out setting fires by simply pouring gasoline on the ground and then setting the gasoline on fire. After almost setting himself on fire, he decided that he needed to start the fires in a different manner. He then developed the device that he used in the vast majority of the fires he set. He used a one-gallon jug filled with gasoline. He wrapped a sock or piece of clothing around the top of the jug and then set it on fire. In this manner, the fire would take some time to ignite, thereby allowing him to escape with ease. He stated that he always carried the jug in a plastic bag to evade detection. He reasoned that if anyone saw him, it would look like he was carrying a bag of groceries rather than a jug of gasoline. Sweatt stated that he picked his targets at random. He further stated that he typically placed the device near a door because it was more likely to burn at that location. He further acknowledged that he was, at times, aware that persons were in the homes at which he set these devices on fire.

During the execution of the search warrant on his home, investigators found seventy-five videotapes, additional marine corps dress pants, a US Navy hat, and a newspaper article on a fatal fire on Montello Street in Washington, DC, in 2002. A review of the recovered tapes revealed many stories referencing fires set by the serial arsonist over the past two years. They also revealed a number of military personnel in uniform and Metro transit drivers in uniform unknowingly being recorded.

Thomas Sweatt eventually confessed to the fires that investigators had linked him to and eventually to more, forty-four in all. On June 6, 2005, fifty-year-old Sweatt pleaded guilty to multiple counts including arson, one count of first-degree murder in the death of Lou Edna Jones on June 5, 2003, and one count of first-degree murder in the death of Mrs. Annie Brown on February 5, 2002. Sweatt was sentenced to life without parole and sent to the US State Penitentiary in Terre Haute, Indiana.

Daley said, "It's a great feeling to be a part of what I consider to be an outstanding team; a team that rallied together when we needed it to. A team that stayed focused in the search for the infamous serial arsonist, and Sweatt takes his dark motive for setting the fires with him to prison." Ultimately, investigators were able to close 353 fires that Thomas Sweatt had confessed to. The most prolific and deadliest arsonist on record is brought down.

Tom wrote, *I was sentenced to life in prison without the possibility of parole, plus 120 years. The judge told me so firmly that I would never be able to hurt anybody ever again. I cried hard and didn't look back at my family (who were all there). The courtroom was packed with news reporters, spectators, family members on both sides, and of course, the victims. They still don't have any closure because I was just a mess and too nervous to talk. But I did glance over at them and told them I was sorry and asked that they turn their hatred into understanding. While at Charles County, I did write to some of the victims' families. They never responded.*

Upon his arrest, DC Mayor Anthony Williams stated, "If you threaten, if you terrorize, if you turn lives upside-down in our community, we're going to hunt you down, we're going to find you, and we're going to bring you to justice and put you behind bars."

Metropolitan Police Department Police Chief Charles Ramsey said, "This guy posed a huge threat to everyone's safety in our region, setting fires at night. We could have very easily had multiple fatalities. That's how serious this was."

Two years later, in 2007, DC-based journalist Dave Jamieson corresponded with Sweatt in prison. Shockingly, in the same article, Sweatt confessed to yet another fire he set in January 1985. Forty-five-year-old Betsie May Duncan and her husband, thirty-eight-year-old Roy Picott suffered severe burns and smoke inhalation. Betsie Mae died that same night. Roy died two months later in an area hospital. Thomas Sweatt's confession adds two more homicides to his gruesome list. Since the night of the fire, twenty years earlier, the official cause of death had been listed as a discarded cigarette, but investigators knew that was wrong. Nobody in the house smoked.

If I had never been caught, I'd still be active. Perhaps the fires would be bigger, and I'd take brave steps. Like, I'd go home to North Carolina to visit, and maybe I'd cruise the town and pick out a nice spot that's full of little single houses with bicycles, a basketball hoop in the backyard, and maybe a car that's been converted into a hot rod. It would let me think that perhaps a son, boyfriend, or husband might live there. I feel confident that DC, Maryland, and Virginia would have played out by now. I would need a new location. The smell of those little houses burning, the sound of fire crackling is...but hoping at the same time nobody gets hurt.

CHAPTER 13

LIFE IN PRISON

*I*t's been so quiet and peaceful in prison lately. Some yell through the locked doors every now and then. I was moved today by a fellow inmate who was just released. Here I am serving a life sentence without parole and have plenty of places to live if I were released. Mr. Riffe, he made parole today and has no family. He needs an address for the FBOP to verify upon getting out. Today he came to me asking a big favor if I could help. So handsome, so young, I couldn't resist. But I did. That's just so sad, and he could have gone home. You can't burn those bridges.

It's funny though. The inmate thinks I'm here because I burned down my lover's house down and he died in it. That story is false. But make no error about it—sex has played a part in going about the business in prison.

I took a mental trip to your firehouse, Engine 22, today! You welcomed me in and gave me a hug. It felt so good, and that was a nice handshake, too. I couldn't help but stare at your uniform. You and the firefighters were cooking. The food smelled so good. They all said hey in a very high-spirited fashion and asked if I wanted to join them for supper. I became shy and tried not to let my feelings show but I was happy to hear that. They laughed out loud, especially the black firefighters. You showed me the lounge room, and that's where I stayed and watched TV. It felt good being in your company—the sergeant and his men at Engine 22. I was hopeful you'd get a call, so I could feel what it's like to ride in a big, red firetruck with the sirens sounding off! That would be awesome. I would sit in the back. I hated to leave after supper and all that, but it was getting late. It was time to go home, and then I woke up. Ah...it was just a dream. But dreams do come true! I'll keep dreaming!

I rarely hear from my blood brothers, except during the holidays. I have a brother who lives in South Carolina, and he has yet to visit. He asked that his name be put on the visitors list. We'll see what happens. Having a relative in prison really takes commitment and true love to keep in touch, otherwise that relationship will slowly fade away. And I'm beginning to feel a little of that. I don't want to be remembered only during Thanksgiving and Christmas. I have another brother, the youngest of all the boys, who has never left North Carolina. He's fifty-three and lives with some young girl who's probably young enough to be his daughter. But that's what he's done all his life. He has two sons. One was in the navy. I asked him to send pictures of him and he did. Sorry to say, I masturbated over my nephew because I liked him in his navy uniform. I'm not ashamed. He calls me baby whenever he's home at my mother's house.

I've heard of a lot of cities in Maryland, but never Huntingtown. That's Southern Maryland, too. I've been through some parts of Southern Maryland and it's really pretty—lots of farms, acres of land with old houses, etc. When I got arrested, I was taken to Charles County Detention Center in La Plata, Maryland. I stayed there for about three months before leaving for Ohio. They put me in isolation II for fear that I'd be attacked by the general population. Things have really gone well so far in prison. Having never been to jail before, this was, and still is, an experience I'll never forget. But there's always the thought that one day some of the victims' relatives will meet me. Some inmates volunteer their time. I don't because it's still fresh and painful.

You asked why I am allowing you to write this book and cooperating with you but no one else. When I first got arrested and spent three months in Charles County jail, my nerves were shot. I thought I was having a heart attack. The nurse simply said, "You are just having an anxiety attack and are depressed." I had never been to jail. So this was really a huge experience.

Writing this story was the furthest thing from my mind. Of course, there were reporters from DC and Maryland writing (the same as you're doing) to come visit and tell my story. I declined. It was just too early, and I wasn't ready for anything of this nature. Jon, I didn't know that I'd survive prison life because the nature of the crimes. Even my family didn't expect me to survive a month. But I guess God was not ready for me yet. It was certainly a bumpy road from the start. Now that six years have passed, things have gotten a little easier. It's still hard to talk about or even write about the fires. There's a long road ahead.

You asked what prison was like in Terre Haute, Indiana. I arrived there on November 2, 2005 (one day before my fifty-first birthday). That's crazy. At that time, it was a good spot. It's like where I'm at now—mostly whites, very few blacks. But what can you expect in Klan Country :)? Sorry, Jon, but that's how it was. The prison ran well until a fight or violence broke out. My first lockdown there was for seventeen days. I thought I'd go crazy. I started having more anxiety attacks and getting depressed. I was lucky enough to have a good "cellie." He helped show me how to do time.

I had (and still have) a strong family support. They sacrificed the long trips, some from North Carolina, to visit. It's not a good spot now. Thank God I left in October 2008. I volunteered to transfer on a medical to Lee County, Virginia (another USP). I stayed there for a year and left in October 2009 to transfer to Coleman, Florida. I just take it one day at a time here. I haven't had any problems. I have managed to stay "clear conduct" thus far. I'm thankful for that. It's just so homophobic. But if you respect yourself, you'll get respect in return.

When I'm sitting in the unit surrounded by a bunch of men, one can't help but wonder what they look like naked! Yes, there's one thing that stays constantly on my mind, and that's sex. But I rarely have sex. I fantasize a lot. One dude who lives on the block, I lust after him, and I pretend that we're drinking wine (he'd be smoking weed and drinking wine) on the sofa beside me. I'd sit in his lap first, then I'd slide on the floor to touch his feet and caress his penis, getting it hard for me to start sucking. I would unstrap his belt and unbutton his khaki brown pants to see his smooth, muscular thighs. I love when he opens and closes his long legs—that really turns me on. Open and close, open and close tight, open wide and close slowly, while patting his shoes (size 13). My thoughts can run wild into crazy, crazy stuff. It's disturbing, and I can't write about it, Jon.

I spend my time reading, writing, and sleeping. I take classes and am studying French right now. Nothing ever changes. It's the same faces every day, same scenery. That's what makes it so boring. Sometimes you must do the things you like best, just for today—then tomorrow, you do it all over again. Sometimes it's just easiest to think about it one day at a time.

Here the staff is mostly black. The warden is black, the captain is black, and they have no problem letting us know who is in power. The prison is a mixture of inmates who are sick medically, can't go anywhere else (they did something wrong at other spots), or dropped off. Not too many hardcore criminals. One man's crime is always worse than the next man's. I haven't had a "cellie" for almost five months, and it's been sweet.

I talked to my sister a couple of days ago, and she told me that this inmate, AKA "Crank," has been designated to come here from another United States Penitentiary. Jon, that's not good news. In 2005, while at Charles County, Maryland, I was transferred to Terre Haute, Indiana. That's where I met him. We were cellies. He taught me how to do time because I was so green and had no clue of how to handle prison. Having said that, my family felt the need to corresponding with him through me. He wrote letters to them. They sent money to him and thought it was just a small price to pay to keep me safe. So that *went on for a while. They felt I needed Crank for protection because of the nature of my crimes (with which I certainly agreed). Some of the inmates knew about the arsonist there. Like I've written in other letters, the people here don't really know the true story of my crime. Crank does to a certain extent. He does know there were some houses that burned and one lady died, Mrs. Lou Edna Jones. But the deep-down story? No, he doesn't know. But he knows something that I'm afraid he'll tell the homies here. Not that anything will happen, but it's the thought some of them will finally learn. More and more, "DC homies" are arriving here. What's going on?! I've grown since those years, and hopefully he'll see that and just let me be.*

ENDING STATEMENT: In 2006, Agents Scott Fulkerson and Bob (from the ATF) came to visit me in Terre Haute. They wanted to ask if there were any other deaths from the fires. I didn't feel the need to tell them anything else, because now it served no purpose. So the answer will always be kept a secret. Tell all the DC, Maryland, and Virginia firefighters, that Tom, the DC arsonist, said, "Hello and what's up?!?!"

Appendix 1

LIST OF ADMITTED FIRES

1. MARCH 8, 2003: 1705 D Street SE, Washington, DC
2. MARCH 25, 2003: 2030 Jasper Street SE, Washington, DC
3. APRIL 1, 2003: 1500 Mystic Avenue, Oxon Hill, Maryland
4. APRIL 8, 2003: 1813 Jarvis Avenue, Oxon Hill, Maryland
5. APRIL 28, 2003: 3708 Fourth Street SE, Washington, DC
6. MAY 10, 2003: 1505 Fenwood Avenue, Oxon Hill, Maryland
7. MAY 15, 2003: 4026 Southern Avenue SE, Washington, DC
8. MAY 17, 2003: 3367 Alden Place NE, Washington, DC
9. MAY 22, 2003: 105 Fifty-Third Street NE, Washington, DC
10. MAY 27, 2003: 2900 Saint Claire Drive, Silver Hill, Maryland
11. JUNE 5, 2003: 2800 Evarts Street NE, Washington, DC
12. JUNE 5, 2003: 1415 Ames Place NE, Washington, DC
13. JUNE 10, 2003: 5038 Drake Place SE, Washington, DC
14. JUNE 13, 2003: 3808 Ellis Street, Capitol Heights, Maryland
15. JUNE 17, 2003: 924 Abel Avenue, Capitol Heights, Maryland
16. JUNE 17, 2003: 5800 Jefferson Heights Drive, Capitol Heights, Maryland
17. JUNE 20, 2003: 1315 Chapel Oaks Drive, Capitol Heights, Maryland
18. JUNE 21, 2003: 2406 Wintergreen Avenue, District Heights, Maryland

19. JUNE 22, 2003: 1505 Ruston Avenue, Capitol Heights, Maryland

20. JUNE 25, 2003: 4920 North Capitol Street NW, Washington, DC

21. JUNE 30, 2003: 2505 Randolph Street NE, Washington, DC. Fire was set on the front porch near the door.

22. JULY 2, 2003: 316 Seventeenth Street SE, Washington, DC

23. SEPTEMBER 4, 2003: 5101 Barnaby Run Drive, Oxon Hill, Maryland. The device was placed at the front door of the house.

24. SEPTEMBER 8, 2003: 202 Quackenbos Street NW, Washington, DC. Fire was started on the front porch near the door and all the devices were found.

25. SEPTEMBER 10, 2003: 4713 Dix Street NE, Washington, DC

26. SEPTEMBER 14, 2003: 4115 Anacostia Avenue NE, Washington, DC. Two men encounter Mr. Sweatt at their residence. He leaves behind his jug with gasoline in it.

27. OCTOBER 8, 2003: 1315 Otis Avenue NE, Washington, DC. The fire was on the front porch at the front door. Investigators from the task force were on the scene before the fire department arrived. The blocks around the scene were sealed off; everyone was stopped and questioned. Zero. The guy vanished again.

28. NOVEMBER 11, 2003: 1700 Twenty-Fourth Street NE, Washington, DC. The device was placed in front of the home near the left-hand corner. All the components were present. Investigators were again quickly on the scene; they arrived as the fire apparatus arrived. Still, they came up with nothing.

29. NOVEMBER 16, 2003: 4410 West Braddock Road, Alexandria, Virginia. The case took a major turn. The arsonist had set thirty-four fires that the task force knew about. Twenty-one of those fires were set in the city and thirteen in Prince George's County. At 0451 hours on a Sunday morning, a fire was set in Alexandria, Virginia, at 4410 West Braddock Road. The home was on the grounds of a nursing home and was where out-of-town nurses lived. In every criminal investigation was a single-family residence on the arson investigations, the turns generally have a more in-depth meaning.

The arsonist usually becomes bored and needs a change to keep up the interest. Was this it? There were now fires in Maryland, DC, and Virginia.

30. DECEMBER 20, 2003: 5702 Eighty-Third Place, New Carrollton, Maryland. At 0437 hours, a fire occurred in the New Carrollton section of PG County. The device was placed at the front of the house by the garage door. What was more interesting was that the fire was about one mile from the task force operation and happened the very day the behavioral profiler said there would have a fire within a week.

31. JANUARY 22, 2004: 3418 Fifty-Fifth Avenue, Bladensburg, Virginia. At 0311 hours, there was another turn with the arsonist. The fire was set in an apartment building, not a single-family home. The device was placed in an interior stairwell but not in such a way that it blocked people from getting out. Interestingly, it was about one mile from the command post but in the opposite direction of the Eighty-Third Street fire. Was the arsonist sending us a message?

32. FEBRUARY 6, 2004: 7101 Richmond Highway, Alexandria, Virginia. The fire took place at a garden apartment complex; a device was found in front of an apartment door directly next to the stairway. This one was blocking people's egress. Luckily, the fire was in the middle of the day and while school was out. Not many people were in the building. Another twist: a fire in the middle of the day and no one is seen. The arsonist seemed to be stepping up his game.

33. FEBRUARY 14, 2004: 7700 Blair Road, Silver Spring, Maryland: This was Valentine's Day. At 0456 hours, a fire took place in Montgomery County, Maryland, another case first. The device was placed in the stairwell between the first and second floors and blocked all passage from the upper stories to the exit. When the fire companies arrived, people were hanging from windows. Several were hurt and had to be rescued. During the evidence collection, a pair of burned black pants was recovered. In an analysis conducted by the Montgomery County Crime Lab, DNA consistent with the DNA of the hair found at 4115 Anacostia Avenue in DC was found on the pants. The task force concluded that the DNA was that of the serial arsonist and welcomed Montgomery County police to the task force.

34. APRIL 16, 2004: 2401 Rosecroft Village Circle, East Oxon Hill, Maryland. All the parts of the device were present, and it was placed on the side of the house next to the front porch. Recovered in the debris was a burned piece of advertisement for a local tax-preparation firm. The task force traced the ad back to a local Giant Food store in Northwest DC.

35. MAY 13, 2004: 3403 Beechcraft Drive, Alexandria, Virginia. The fire occurred at 0438 hours at a single-family home. All the components of our device were present; it was placed at the front-left side of the house.

36. AUGUST 30, 2004: 4012 Elmwood Drive, Alexandria, Virginia. The device was placed directly in front of the entrance door. Luckily, the occupant had already left for work. There was a remarkable likeness to the surroundings of this home and that of the home on Beachcraft. Both homes were at the end of a block, both were backed up to woods, and both had a creek running beside them. There was a park nearby and new homes under construction in the rear. The homes were single story and had the same style landscape.

37. SEPTEMBER 8, 2004: 2800 Channing Street NE, Washington, DC. The device was located under the driver's side front wheel. The vehicle was owned by a Metro transit bus driver and was parked across the street from a transit bus barn. There were no cars in the case that we knew of to this point, but this fire caused us to wonder about how many fires our arsonist might have been setting that we did not know about.

38. SEPTEMBER 17, 2004: 6302 Forty-Ninth Avenue, Riverdale, Maryland

39. SEPTEMBER 20, 2004: 2804 Thirtieth Street, Washington, DC. The fire was one block from a fire at 2800 Evarts Street, which took place on June 5, 2003. This fire took the life Ms. Lou Edna Jones and was confirmed as the work of the arsonist. The fire was also two blocks from Channing Street car fire twelve days before. Recovered at the fire was a piece of cloth wick, which was later determined to be consistent with an athletic sock.

40. SEPTEMBER 23, 2004: 10817 Amherst Avenue, Wheaton,

Maryland. The device was placed in front of a garage in a townhouse development. The arsonist was very busy and had us moving from one county to another state. Then, with no reasoning, fifty-one days passed without another fire being set.

41. NOVEMBER 8, 2004: 6968 Walker Mill Road, District Heights, Maryland

42. DECEMBER 5, 2004: 301 N. Bryan St, Arlington, Virginia. The fire was set on a rear deck of a single-family home. The fire involved what investigators believed was a candle wrapped in a cloth and then soaked with gasoline. In the canvass of the scene, investigators located a US Marine Corps dress cap and a pair of Marine Corps dress pants. These items were found on the block next to the fire. It was safe to collect the evidence and have it reviewed by the lab.

43. DECEMBER 6, 2004: 5055 Eleventh Street NE, Washington, DC. Vehicle fire located about two miles from Channing, Thirtieth, and Evarts locations. The owner was a Metro employee. The device was found under the front passenger's side wheel. During the review, investigators found some writing on a plastic bag: "Made in China for the Cornelius Shop." Based on this, investigators located a Cornelius Shoppe in England.

44. DECEMBER 7, 2004: 4205 Fifty-Third Avenue, Bladensburg, Maryland. The device was in the stairwell between the first and second floors, blocking all passage from the upper floors.

45. DECEMBER 10, 2004: 3021 Yost Place NE, Washington, DC. Device (with black bag) found on front porch directly next to the front door. It was determined that the bags were distributed to Circle Seven, owned by the same person (two locations in DC). Video surveillance was established.

46. IN ADDITION to the above-listed residential fires, Sweatt also set fires to vehicles parked at a parking lot at Eighth and I streets, Washington, DC, on February 4, 2003; February 25, 2003; February 26, 2003; and March 3, 2003.

Appendix 2

COURT TRANSCRIPT OF GUILTY PLEA

Transcript of Guilty Plea: June 6, 2005

UNITED STATES OF AMERICA
VS.
THOMAS A. SWEATT

BEFORE THE HONORABLE DEBORAH K. CHASANOW

APPEARANCES:

ON BEHALF OF THE GOVERNMENT:
MYTHILI T. RAMAN, ESQ.
JAMES M. TRUSTY, ESQ.
ASSISTANT US ATTORNEYS

ON BEHALF OF THE DEFENDANT:
JOHN CHAMBLE, ESQ.

THE COURT: Good afternoon. Please be seated. Ms. Raman.

MS. RAMAN: Calling the case of United States of America vs. Thomas Sweatt, Mythili T. Raman and Jim Trusty on behalf of the United States. We're joined at counsel table by Special Agent Scott Fulkerson and Tom Daley of ATF and Jennifer Anderson of the District and also Assistant US Attorney Morris Parker from the Eastern District of Virginia.

MR. CHAMBLE: Good afternoon, Your Honor. On behalf of Thomas Sweatt, John Chamble, ready for proceeding.

THE COURT: All right. We're here for the arraignment of Thomas Sweatt on charges that are contained in informations filed in three different jurisdictions. Two were transferred here from the District of Columbia and from Virginia. They have now all been consolidated under the case number that Ms. Raman announced a moment ago.

Mr. Sweatt, we need to begin by asking you to stand and address your attention to Ms. Fosbrook. She's going to place you under oath and ask you some preliminary questions. (The oath was administered.)

THE CLERK: You may put your hand down. Please state your full name for the record.

THE DEFENDANT: Thomas Anthony Sweatt.

THE CLERK: What is your age?

THE DEFENDANT: Fifty.

THE CLERK: What is your date of birth?

THE DEFENDANT: 1954.

THE CLERK: Thank you.

THE COURT: You may be seated. Mr. Sweatt, you are charged in three informations: one from Maryland, one from the District of Columbia, and one from Virginia. I am now going to read you the charges contained in each of those informations, and I am going to advise you as to the maximum possible penalty for each of those offenses as we go through them. Do you have a copy of the information from the District of Maryland in front of you?

THE DEFENDANT: Yes.

THE COURT: Okay. Count 1 charges that on or about February 14, 2004, here in Maryland, you did maliciously damage and destroy and attempt to damage and destroy, by means of fire, a building, specifically the apartment building located at 7700 Blair Road, Silver Spring, Maryland, which was a building used in interstate commerce and in an activity affecting interstate commerce, as a result of which personal injury resulted to persons. That charge is alleged to have been in violation of Title 18 US Code section 844(i).

That charge, which covers activity of maliciously damaging or destroying or attempting to damage or destroy by means of fire or explosive any building used in interstate commerce or in an activity affecting interstate commerce, because it also alleges injury to people, carries a minimum mandatory sentence of seven years in prison, a possible maximum penalty of forty years in prison.

The imprisonment can be followed by up to five years of supervised release. There is a possibility of a $250,000 fine, a $100 special assessment, and an order to pay restitution. Do you understand that charge?

THE DEFENDANT: Yes.

THE COURT: And the maximum penalty and the mandatory minimum that applies?

THE DEFENDANT: Yes.

THE COURT: All right. Let me advise you that supervised release is when someone who has served a period in prison is released on conditions of good behavior. If he violates those conditions, he can be sentenced to an additional time in prison, on top of whatever was imposed to begin with and without any credit for time spent on release. Do you understand that aspect of supervised release?

THE DEFENDANT: Yes.

THE COURT: Count 2 of the information, here in Maryland, charges that on or about February 14, 2004, here in Maryland, you did knowingly possess a firearm as defined in Title 26, United States Code section 5845(a), specifically a destructive device, which was not registered to you in the National Firearms Registration and Transfer Record, and that possession was at 7700 Blair Road, Silver Spring, Maryland.

That charge is alleged to have been in violation of Title 26, US Code section 5861(d) and section 5871.

The possible penalty for the charge in Count 2 of this information is ten years in prison, three years of supervised release, a $10,000 fine, and an additional $100 special assessment.

That statute makes it unlawful for any person to receive or possess a firearm which is not registered to him in the National Firearms Registration and Transfer Record. For purposes of this statue, the term firearm includes a destructive device, which includes any incendiary device.

Do you understand the charge in Count 2 and the maximum possible penalty for that charge?

THE DEFENDANT: Yes.

THE COURT: Count 3 of the Maryland information charges that on or about February 14, 2004, here in Maryland, you did knowingly possess a firearm, to wit, a destructive device, in furtherance of a crime of violence for which you may be prosecuted in a court of the United States, that is, the offense charged in Count 1 of this information, to wit, arson in violation of Title 18 US Code section 844(i).

This charge is alleged in violation of Title 18 US Code section 924(c) (1) (A) and (B) (ii). This statute, which makes it a separate crime for any person who during and in relation to any crime of violence for which the person may be prosecuted in a court of the United States, to use or carry a firearm or, in furtherance of a crime, to possess a firearm, shall be sentenced in addition to the penalty for the underlying crime of violence.

The first charge of the 924(c) violation, which charges that you possessed a destructive device, carries a mandatory thirty-year sentence in prison, a maximum of life in prison, can be followed with five years of supervised release, $250,000 fine, and another special assessment of $100.

The law provides that the sentence for this offense must be consecutive to any other term of imprisonment imposed for the underlying crime of violence. Do you understand the charge in Count 3, as well as the mandatory consecutive minimum sentence that applies?

THE DEFENDANT: Yes.

THE COURT: Count 4 charges that on or about April 16, 2004, here in Maryland, you did knowingly possess a firearm as defined in Title 26, United States Code Section 5845(a), specifically a destructive device which was not registered to you in the National Firearms Registration and Transfer Record, at 2401 Rosecroft Village Circle East, in Oxon Hill, Maryland.

This is another charge of possession of an unregistered destructive device, and as I've told you, this type of charge carries a possible penalty of ten years in prison, three years of supervised release, a $10,000 fine, and a $100 special assessment. Do you understand the charge and the possible penalty in Count 4?

THE DEFENDANT: Yes.

THE COURT: Count 5 charges that on or about December 7, 2004, here in Maryland, you did maliciously damage and destroy and attempt to damage and destroy by means of fire a building, specifically the apartment building located at 4205 Fifty-Third Avenue in Bladensburg, Maryland, which was a building used in interstate commerce and in an activity affecting interstate commerce.

This is another charge under Title 18, US Code section 844(i), but in this one there is no allegation of personal injury. Accordingly, the mandatory minimum sentence would be five years in prison, possible maximum penalty of twenty years in prison, five years of supervised release, $250,000 fine, and another $100 special assessment. Do you understand the charge in Count 5, as well as the mandatory minimum and possible maximum sentence?

THE DEFENDANT: Yes.

THE COURT: Count six in the Maryland information charges that on or about December 7, 2004, here in Maryland, you did knowingly possess a firearm as defined in Title 26 United States Code section 5845(a), specifically a destructive device which was not registered to you in the National Firearms Registration and Transfer Record, and that this possession took place at 4205 Fifty-Third Avenue, in Bladensburg, Maryland.

This is an additional charge of possession of the unregistered destructive device. It carries a possible penalty of ten years in prison, three years of supervised release, a $10,000 fine, and an additional $100 special assessment. Do you understand the charge and the possible penalty for Count 6?

THE DEFENDANT: Yes.

THE COURT: Do you have a copy of the information from the District of Columbia in front of you?

THE DEFENDANT: Yes.

THE COURT: Count 1 charges that on or about October 8, 2003, within the District of Columbia, the defendant, Thomas Sweatt, did maliciously damage and destroy, and attempt to damage and destroy by means of fire, a building located at 1315 Otis Street NE, Washington, DC, which was used in interstate commerce and in an activity affecting interstate commerce.

This, again, is an arson charge under 18 US Code Section 844(i). There is no allegation in this charge of personal injury. Accordingly, it carries a mandatory minimum five-year sentence and a maximum of twenty years, five years of supervised release, $250,000 fine, and a $100 special assessment.

Again, do you understand the charge in Count 1 of the District of Columbia information, along with the mandatory minimum and possible maximum sentence?

THE DEFENDANT: Yes.

THE COURT: Count 2 charges that on or about October 8, 2003, within the District of Columbia, you used and carried a firearm that is a destructive device, more specifically, an incendiary bomb and similar device, during and in relation to a crime of violence for which you may be prosecuted in a court of the United States.

The offense charged in Count 1 of this information is the arson charge. This is an additional charge of use or possession of a firearm during a crime of violence under 18 US Code Section 924(c). Because this is the second such offense charged in this series of indictments, it carries a mandatory life sentence.

This sentence must be imposed, to be served consecutive to any sentence imposed for the underlying crime of violence; that is the arson charged in Count 1. Do you understand the charge in Count 2 of the District of Columbia information, as well as the mandatory life sentence, consecutive to the other sentence that is applicable here?

THE DEFENDANT: Yes.

THE COURT: Count 3 of the District of Columbia information charges that on or about October 8, 2003, within the District of Columbia, you did possess a firearm; that is a destructive device, more specifically an incendiary bomb and similar device, which was not registered to you in the National Firearms Registration and Transfer Record.

This is an additional charge under Title 26 US Code section

5861(d) and 5871, carries a possible sentence of ten years in prison, three years of supervised release, $10,000 fine, and a $100 special assessment. Do you understand the charge and possible sentence for Count 2 of the District of Columbia information?

THE DEFENDANT: Yes.

THE COURT: Count 4 is an additional charge of possession of an unregistered firearm. It alleges that on or about September 14, 2003, within the District of Columbia, you did possess a firearm, that is a destructive device, more specifically an incendiary bomb and similar device, which was not registered to you in the National Firearms Registration and Transfer Record.

Again, the possible penalty for this charge in Count 4 is ten years in prison, three years of supervised release, a $10,000 fine, and a $100 special assessment. Do you understand the charge and the possible penalty for Count 4?

THE DEFENDANT: Yes.

THE COURT: Count 5 charges again possession of an unregistered firearm. It reads on or about September 20, 2004, within the District of Columbia, you did receive and possess a firearm; that is a destructive device, more specifically an incendiary bomb and similar device that was not registered to you in the National Firearms Registration and Transfer Record.

Once again, this charge carries a possible ten years in prison, followed by three years of supervised release, a $10,000 fine, and a $100 special assessment. Do you understand the possible penalty as well as the charge in Count 5?

THE DEFENDANT: Yes.

THE COURT: Count 6 charges that on or about June 5, 2003, you, within the District of Columbia, while armed with an incendiary device, in perpetrating and attempting to perpetrate the crime of arson, killed Lou Edna Jones, by setting fire to 2800 Evarts Street NE, thereby causing injuries from which Lou Edna Jones died.

This is a charge of first degree murder while armed, felony murder, in violation of DC Code Title 22 sections 2101, 4502. That section of the DC Code applies to whoever being of sound memory and discretion, kills another, either purposely by deliberate or premeditated malice, or in perpetrating or attempting to perpetrate an offense punishable by imprisonment, or without purpose to do so, kills another in perpetrating or attempting to perpetrate any arson as that offense is defined under District of Columbia law. Do you understand that charge?

THE DEFENDANT: Yes.

THE COURT: That charge in Count 6 carries a mandatory thirty-year sentence, minimum sentence of thirty years, a maximum sentence of sixty years in prison, could be followed with five years of supervised release, and there is a $100 special assessment.

Do you understand both the mandatory minimum and the possible maximum sentence you face under Count 6 of the District of Columbia information?

THE DEFENDANT: Yes.

THE COURT: Count 7 of the District of Columbia information charges that on or about February 5, 2002, you, within the District of Columbia, with the intent to kill another and to inflict serious bodily injury on another, and with a conscious disregard of an extreme risk of death and serious bodily injury to another, caused the death of Annie Brown by setting fire to 1210 Montello Avenue NE, while armed with an incendiary device, thereby causing injuries from which Annie Brown died on or about February 14, 2002.

This is a charge of second degree murder while armed, in violation of 22 DC Code sections 2103 and 4502. Do you understand the charge in Count 7 of the District of Columbia information?

THE DEFENDANT: Yes.

THE COURT: Okay. This charge carries a possible forty-year maximum sentence in prison, five years of supervised release, and an additional $100 special assessment. Do you understand the maximum penalty for Count 7?

THE DEFENDANT: Yes.

THE COURT: Do you have the information from the Eastern District of Virginia before you? Do you have a copy of that Mr. Sweatt?

THE DEFENDANT: Yes.

THE COURT: This one charges in Count 1, that on or about November 16, 2003, in Alexandria, Virginia, in the Eastern District of Virginia, you did maliciously damage, by means of a fire, a building located at 4410 West Braddock Road, Alexandria, Virginia, which was the cottage of a nursing care facility operated by the Church of Christian Science, and which was used in interstate commerce and in an activity affecting interstate commerce.

This is again alleged in violation of Title 18 US Code section 844(i). There is no allegation of personal injury with regard to this, so the five-year mandatory minimum applies, maximum of twenty years in prison, five years of supervised release, a $250,000 fine, and an additional $100 special assessment. You understand the charge in Count 1 of the Virginia information, the mandatory minimum that applies, and the possible maximum sentence?

THE DEFENDANT: Yes.

THE COURT: Count 2 charges that on or about February 6, 2004, in Fairfax County, Virginia, in the Eastern District of Virginia, you did maliciously damage, by means of fire, an apartment building located at 1701 Richmond Highway, Alexandria, Virginia, which was used in interstate commerce and in an activity affecting interstate commerce, as a result of which personal injury resulted to a person, specifically Ann Daniels.

This is an allegation under Title 18 US Code section 844(i) with an allegation of personal injury. Accordingly, the mandatory minimum sentence is seven years in prison, possible maximum sentence of forty years in prison, followed by five years of supervised release, a $250,000 fine, and an additional $100 special assessment. Do you understand the charge, the mandatory minimum, and the possible maximum sentence for Count 2 in this information?

THE DEFENDANT: Yes.

THE COURT: All of the above possible sentences can be imposed to run consecutively, that is one after another. The two sentences under the 924(c) counts, as I have already told you, are required to be imposed to be served consecutively.

Supervised release terms are usually imposed to run concurrently, that is at the same time, but there is no requirement that they be imposed in that fashion.

The fines, if imposed, can be aggregated, that is, added together. The special assessments, however, that is the $100 on each of the counts, must be imposed separately for each of the counts.

In addition to the penalties that I have just talked about, the Court can impose a restitution judgment. That is a money judgment against you, requiring you to pay the victims of these offenses for certain of their expenses.

Do you understand all of these aspects of the possible penalties that you face by virtue of the charges contained in the three separate informations?

THE DEFENDANT: Yes.

THE COURT: Okay. You have had an initial appearance on a Complaint alleging some of these offenses, and at that time you were advised of your right to remain silent concerning the charges. Do you recall that advice you received?

THE DEFENDANT: Yes.

THE COURT: Okay. With regard to all of the charges that I have just read to you, that advice regarding your right to remain silent applies equally to all of them. Do you understand that?

THE DEFENDANT: Yes.

THE COURT: In addition, you, of course, have the right to be represented by an attorney, whether you're in court for a hearing like we're having now, or there is an interview or any kind of proceeding outside of the courtroom. You understand your right to be represented by counsel?

THE DEFENDANT: Yes.

THE COURT: Okay. Mr. Chamble, of course, is here today and will be representing you fully on all three of these informations that now have been transferred here and consolidated together. With regard to the initial complaint filed here in Maryland, there was an Order of Detention filed after a hearing before the Magistrate Judge. That remains in place and will now apply to all of those charges. Are we ready to move to the formal arraignment portion?

MR. CHAMBLE: We're prepared, Your Honor.

THE COURT: Ms. Fosbrook.

THE CLERK: Will the defendant please rise. Mr. Sweatt, have you been furnished with copies of the information's?

THE DEFENDANT: Yes.

THE CLERK: Have you read the informations?

THE DEFENDANT: Yes.

THE CLERK: Do you understand the charges that have been placed against you?

THE DEFENDANT: Yes.

THE CLERK: Mr. Chamble, you represent the defendant?

MR. CHAMBLE: I do.

THE CLERK: Are you satisfied that the defendant understands what he is charged with?

MR. CHAMBLE: I am.

THE CLERK: Mr. Sweatt, you have been charged with a six-count information in the District of the Maryland. What is your plea?

THE DEFENDANT: Guilty to each and every count.

THE CLERK: The plea is guilty as to the six-count information in the District of Maryland, is that correct?

THE DEFENDANT: That's correct.

THE CLERK: Mr. Sweatt, you have been charged in a seven-count information in the District of Columbia. What is your plea?

THE DEFENDANT: Guilty to each and every count.

THE CLERK: The plea is guilty to the seven-count information in the District of Columbia, is that correct?

THE DEFENDANT: Yes.

THE CLERK: Mr. Sweatt, you've been charged in a two-count information in the Eastern District of Virginia. What is your plea?

THE DEFENDANT: Guilty.

THE CLERK: The plea is guilty to the two-count information in the Eastern District of Virginia, is that right?

THE DEFENDANT: Yes.

THE CLERK: Thank you. You may be seated.

THE COURT: Mr. Sweatt, I need to ask you some additional

questions, because I must make certain that you understand fully what it means to plead guilty and that you are doing so voluntarily. If any of my questions are unclear, would you let me know?

THE DEFENDANT: Yes.

THE COURT: Okay. And if you want to ask Mr. Chamble anything as we go forward, you certainly may do that as well. Please tell me your educational background.

THE DEFENDANT: I completed high school at Roanoke Rapids Junior\Senior High School, in Roanoke Rapids, North Carolina. I also went to Halifax Community College for one year and a half.

THE COURT: Okay. I assume you have no difficulty reading and writing in English, is that correct?

THE DEFENDANT: That's correct.

THE COURT: Have you ever received any treatment for any mental illness, alcoholism, or any drug problem?

THE DEFENDANT: No.

THE COURT: Are you currently taking any medications that can make you drowsy or interfere with your concentration?

THE DEFENDANT: I'm taking medication where I'm at right now.

THE COURT: You are? For pain or what kind of—

THE DEFENDANT: High blood pressure.

THE COURT: Do those medications make you drowsy or interfere with your concentration?

THE DEFENDANT: No.

THE COURT: Okay. Physically, are you feeling all right at the moment?

THE DEFENDANT: No.

THE COURT: No. You're nervous, I'm certain.

THE DEFENDANT: Yes.

THE COURT: Okay. Do you understand what I'm talking to you about and able to answer my questions all right?

THE DEFENDANT: Yes.

THE COURT: Okay. I understand you're nervous, but other than that, are you feeling all right physically?

THE DEFENDANT: I'll be okay.

THE COURT: You'll be all right. All right. If you want to take a drink of water, relax, take a deep breath. I know we're talking about very important and serious things, and you need to be able to talk with me and understand what I'm asking you.

THE DEFENDANT: Thank you.

THE COURT: Okay. Mr. Chamble, do you know of any reason we cannot go forward with this plea?

MR. CHAMBLE: We have no reasons, Your Honor.

THE COURT: Mr. Sweatt, by pleading guilty in this fashion you are giving up quite a number of rights that you would otherwise enjoy under our Constitution and the rules that are applicable.

I'm going to review them with you now to make certain that you understand that if I accept your pleas, you will be giving up all of these rights under the criminal justice system.

First of all, the documents that I read to you are contained in informations. Those are charging documents that were prepared by the prosecutors; that is the United States Attorneys in each of the three jurisdictions, because that prosecuting authority believes that there is probable cause to believe that you committed these offenses.

You have the right not to be prosecuted unless there is an indictment. That is a charging document that only can be filed if a Grand Jury considers evidence presented by the prosecutor and that body decides that there is probable cause to believe that a defendant committed the offense.

A Grand Jury is a group of citizens, up to twenty-three in number, who meet together to consider the evidence presented by the Government and then they vote to determine whether there is probable cause.

Do you understand your right not to be prosecuted unless there is an indictment after a Grand Jury proceeding?

THE DEFENDANT: Yes.

THE COURT: Okay. I have here a document entitled Waiver of Indictment that recites that you understand that you have been charged with the offenses that I just reviewed to you, and that you have decided to give up, that is waive your right to an indictment, and you agree to be prosecuted on the basis of these informations. Is that correct?

THE DEFENDANT: Yes.

THE COURT: Once a person is properly charged with an

offense, that person has the absolute right to plead not guilty. No one can make you come in here and enter a guilty plea. Do you understand that?

THE DEFENDANT: Yes.

THE COURT: If you plead not guilty, you are presumed innocent. That means that you cannot be found guilty unless there is a trial at which your guilt is proven beyond a reasonable doubt.

You have the right to a trial before a jury of twelve people, and all of them would have to agree unanimously that you were guilty. If even one of those jurors did not find guilt, there could be no verdict of guilty at the conclusion of that jury trial.

Now, if you and the government agreed for there to be a trial before a judge without a jury, but in either case you would be presumed innocent and it would be the Government's burden to try to overcome that presumption with proof beyond a reasonable doubt.

To try to do that, the Government would have to call people to testify as witnesses. They would appear in open court. You would be present. They would be placed under oath and they would be subject to cross-examination—that is, questioning by your lawyer.

As I have just advised, you, of course, would have the right to be represented by a lawyer throughout the trial. And, as you know, if you cannot afford to hire counsel, the court appoints an attorney to represent you.

At any trial, you would have the right to testify on your own behalf if you wanted to, but you would have the equal right to remain silent. If you decided not to testify, neither the jury nor the judge could hold it against you in any way, and if you wished, the judge would tell the jury that you have the right not to testify and that they can't hold it against you in any way during their deliberations.

You would have the right to present a defense; that is, to call other people to testify as witnesses, and to produce documents or other things as exhibits, and to have the court's assistance through the subpoena power in requiring people to come to court to testify for you.

If you were found guilty after that trial, you would have the right to appeal, to complain about any mistakes that might have been made before or during that trial. Do you understand all of those rights that you give up by pleading guilty?

THE DEFENDANT: Yes.

THE COURT: If I accept your plea, there will be no trial, and instead we'll move right on to sentencing. Do you understand that?

THE DEFENDANT: Yes.

THE COURT: There is a written plea agreement in this case. Ms. Fosbrook, do you have the original?

THE CLERK: Yes, Your Honor.

THE COURT: Okay. If you could, please walk it over to Mr. Sweatt. I want to ask you, Mr. Sweatt, if you will acknowledge that the signature that appears at the end of the plea and at the end of the Statement of Facts is indeed yours. Are both of those signatures yours, Mr. Sweatt?

THE DEFENDANT: Yes.

THE COURT: This plea agreement was negotiated by Mr. Chamble on your behalf directly with the prosecuting authorities. I have not been a party to those discussions, and I am not bound by this agreement.

I will take it into account as I make sentencing decisions, but you need to understand that I might not agree with all of the proposed advisory guideline findings or any other aspect of this agreement.

You will not be allowed to withdraw your guilty plea, no matter what decisions I make at the time of sentencing. Is that clear?

THE DEFENDANT: Yes.

THE COURT: Okay. We do need to review this document carefully together. It is important that we both understand all of the provisions of the agreement, so we're going to review it in some detail.

First of all, it tells me that you have agreed to waive your right to be charged by an indictment, as you have already done, and that you have agreed to plead guilty to the informations that were pending against you in different jurisdictions.

It sets forth the charges that you understand that you are facing by virtue of those informations. The plea letter then tells me that you understand what the elements of each of these offenses are. These are the things that the Government would have to prove beyond a reasonable doubt if the case were to go to trial.

First, with regard to the charges under 26 US Code section 5861, the elements are, first, that you possessed a firearm as that term is defined in 26 US Code section 5845(a) specifically as a destructive device.

Second, that that firearm was not registered to you in the National Firearms Registration and Transfer Record. And, third, that you acted knowingly.

With regard to the charges under 18 US Code Section 844(i), first, that you damaged or destroyed, or attempted to damage or destroy, a building by means of fire.

Second, that you acted intentionally or with willful disregard of the likelihood that damage or injury would result from your acts. With regard to some of the offenses, that personal injury resulted to any person as a direct or proximate result of your conduct.

And, fourth, that the building that was damaged or destroyed or attempted to be damaged or destroyed, was used in or used in an activity affecting interstate commerce.

With regard to the charges under 18 US Code section 924(c), the Government would have to prove first that you committed a crime of violence for which you may be prosecuted in a court of the United States. In both of these cases it was arson in violation of US Code section 844(i).

Second, that you possessed a destructive device in furtherance of that crime of violence. And, third, that you acted knowingly.

The elements of the charge under 22 DC Code section 2101 are, first, that you caused the death of the decedent and, second, that you did so while committing or attempting to commit arson.

For this offense, the Government need not prove that you specifically intended to kill the decedent. Any killings, even if done without specific intend to kill, and even if accidental, is murder in the first degree if done in committing or attempting to commit arson.

And, finally, the elements of the charge under 22 DC Code section 2103, would be that you caused the death of the decedent and, second, that at the time you did so, you had the specific intend to kill or seriously injure the decedent, or acted in conscious disregard of an extreme risk of death or serious bodily injury to the decedent.

Do you understand those elements that the Government would have to prove beyond a reasonable doubt if any of these charges went to trial?

THE DEFENDANT: Yes.

THE COURT: The plea letter then sets forth the penalties that you face by virtue of these charges. It sets out both the mandatory minimum sentences, as well as the possible maximum sentences that I just reviewed with you in detail at the beginning of these proceedings.

The plea letter also says that you understand that I can order restitution in the full amount of the total actual loss caused by the offense conduct set forth in the stipulation that we will get to in a few moments.

As part of your plea agreement you have agreed to disclose fully to the Probation Officer and to the Court all information concerning finances, bank records, financial records, and all funds that might be available to make restitution. Do you understand that you have made that agreement?

THE DEFENDANT: Yes.

THE COURT: The plea letter then sets forth in writing all of the rights that you will be giving up by pleading guilty that I just reviewed with you here in court.

The plea letter then says that you understand that a sentencing guideline range for this case will be determined by me pursuant to the Sentencing Reform Act. You understand that I will impose a sentence under that Act and take into account this advisory guideline range.

I, obviously, take it into account, but also consider other information in determining what a reasonable sentence will be. You also understand that I may use the District of Columbia Sentencing Commissions Voluntarily Sentencing Guidelines in imposing the sentence for the two murder charges contained in the Information that was transferred here from the District of Columbia.

The plea letter tells me that you and the Government have agreed that neither party, neither you nor the Prosecutor, will seek an upward or downward departure outside of the applicable guideline range pertaining to those two murder charges.

Do you understand both that I will use advisory guidelines, both the federal guidelines and the DC guidelines, in determining the proper sentence?

THE DEFENDANT: Yes.

THE COURT: And do you understand that both you and the Prosecutor have agreed not to ask me to depart with regard to the murder charges under the DC advisory guidelines. Do you understand that?

THE DEFENDANT: Yes.

THE COURT: What follows in the plea agreement are some

factual and advisory guideline stipulations. We're now going to turn to the Prosecutors, and I am going to ask them to read out loud the factual stipulation, which is Attachment A to this plea letter.

Please listen carefully. When they have finished reading these facts, I am going to ask if you agree that these facts are true. Okay. Ms. Raman.

MS. RAMAN: Your Honor, the parties hereby stipulate and agree that if this case had proceeded to trial, the Government would have proven the following facts beyond a reasonable doubt.

The parties also stipulate and agree that the following facts do not encompass all of the evidence that would have been presented had this matter proceeded to trial.

Beginning in February 2003, and continuing through December of 2004, the defendant, Thomas Sweatt, willfully and deliberately set a series of fires in Maryland, the District of Columbia, and Virginia, understanding that his actions would result in damage and injury to persons and property.

The defendant set the fires using incendiary devices, the components of which were a one-gallon polyethylene plastic jug, a polyethylene plastic bag, and a cloth material used as a wick.

A gas chromatograph-mass spectrometry utilized by the Bureau of Alcohol, Tobacco, Firearms, and Explosives laboratory revealed that gasoline was utilized as an accelerant in the devices.

The laboratory also determined that the devices used by the defendant meet the definition of an incendiary device within the meaning of Title 26, United States Code, Sections 5861(d) and 5845.

THE COURT: Do you agree that all of those facts are true?

THE DEFENDANT: Yes.

THE COURT: Do you agree that you are in fact guilty of all of the offenses set forth in the three informations that I read you at the beginning of today's proceeding?

THE DEFENDANT: Yes.

THE COURT: Based upon those facts and the parties' understanding of the guidelines, they have reached some agreements with regard to the advisory guidelines that I should apply.

Once again, Mr. Sweatt, I am not bound by these stipulations, although I will take them into account as I make sentencing findings. First of all, the parties agree that with regard to 18 US Code section 844(i) and 26 US Code 5861, because one of the arsons committed by the defendant in the District of Columbia resulted in the death of the occupant of the home and therefore is felony murder, and because that fatal arson is included in the defendant's relevant conduct for purposes of determining the guideline range, that the base offense level for all of the alleged violations of 844(i) is forty-three. Similarly, the base offense level for the violations of 28 US Code 5816 is also forty-three.

The parties agree that the charged arsons are not supposed to be grouped, because under the guidelines there are different victims in each arson. Nevertheless, the parties agree that it is not necessary to engage in the grouping analysis for purposes of the plea agreement, because the parties agree that the base offense level is forty-three, which is already the highest offense level available under the Federal Sentencing Guidelines.

At this time the Prosecutors do not oppose a two-level

reduction in the offense level, based upon the defendant's prompt recognition and affirmative acceptance of personal responsibility. And, in addition, the Prosecutors will make a motion for an additional one-level downward adjustment based upon him timely notification to plead guilty.

Mr. Sweatt, I say that's how they feel right now. They will pay attention to your conduct up until the time of the sentencing. If at any time you have failed to admit each and every item in the factual stipulation; if you deny your involvement in the offense; if you give conflicting statements about your involvement; if you are untruthful with me, with the Prosecutors, or with the Probation Office; if you obstruct or attempt to obstruct justice prior to sentencing; if you engage in any new criminal conduct prior to sentencing; or if you attempt to withdraw your guilty plea, then the Prosecutors will no longer agree that you are entitled to a three-level downward adjustment for acceptance of responsibility.

If they should do that, I will hear fully from both sides and then I will decide whether or not you have accepted responsibility and what to do about it under the guidelines. Do you understand the procedures that are followed in that case?

THE DEFENDANT: Yes.

THE COURT: With regard to the violations of 18 US Code section 924(c), the parties agree that the defendant must serve a mandatory term of life imprisonment, based upon his plea of guilty to the two counts alleged under the 924(c) violations.

The parties agree that this life sentence must be served consecutively to the sentence for the predicate violations; that is the two arsons under 844(i). With regard to the—is it twenty-one or twenty-two for the District?

MS. ANDERSON: It's twenty-two, Your Honor.

THE COURT: It's twenty-two. Okay. There is just a typo here. With regard to the District of Columbia charges under 22 DC Code section 2101, with regard to first degree murder, the parties agree that this is a group-one offense, that the defendant must serve a mandatory term of imprisonment of thirty years, based upon the plea of guilty.

Absent aggravating circumstances, the maximum sentence that can be imposed, this says forty years, but I advised him it should be sixty.

MS. ANDERSON: That's a typo, Your Honor. It should be sixty.

THE COURT: It should be sixty, which I advised you at the beginning. Under the District of Columbia Sentencing Voluntary Sentencing Commission's Voluntary Sentencing Guidelines, the parties agree that there is a presumption that any sentence imposed will be consecutive to any other sentence, if the other sentences are for crimes involving different victims.

With regard to DC Code section 2103, which is a second-degree murder count, the parties agree that this is under group two and that absent aggravating circumstances the maximum sentence that can be imposed is forty years' imprisonment.

I just read to you the stipulations you have reached with the Prosecutors with regard to those preliminary issues under the guidelines. Do you understand that you have agreed to those guideline applications?

THE DEFENDANT: Yes.

THE COURT: You understand that there has been no agreement between you and the Government with regard to your criminal history information, your criminal history category. That obviously can affect where on a sentencing guideline scale your conduct will fall.

You understand there is no agreement with regard to that aspect of the sentencing guidelines and that means that I will obviously not make a decision until sentencing, when I have seen the information in the Presentence Report and been able to hear from both sides. Do you understand that?

THE DEFENDANT: Yes.

THE COURT: The Government and the defendant agree with respect to the advisory guideline range calculations that there are no other offense characteristics, sentencing guidelines factors, potential departures, or any adjustments set forth in chapters two, three or four of the United States sentencing guidelines. You understand that you are giving up your right to ask me to use any other information, other than what we have just talked about, to decide what the advisory guideline range should be under the federal guidelines. Do you understand that?

THE DEFENDANT: Yes.

THE COURT: Both sides, all parties reserve the right to bring to my attention at the time of sentencing all relevant information concerning the defendant's background, character, and conduct.

Mr. Sweatt, another part of your agreement is that you have agreed to participate in an off-the-record debriefing about all the arsons about which law enforcement officers choose to inquire. You agree as part of that debriefing to provide complete, truthful, and candid information to federal, state, and local investigators regarding any fire that you have set or in which you have been involved, either directly or indirectly. You understand you have made that promise as part twenty-three of your agreement?

THE DEFENDANT: Yes.

THE COURT: The parties have further agreed to the following waiver of appeal rights; because the defendant faces a minimum term of life imprisonment, both the defendant and the Government expressly waive, that is, give up all of their rights to appeal whatever sentence is imposed, including any fine, supervised release, or order of restitution. Do you understand that both sides are giving up all of their rights to appeal my sentencing decisions?

THE DEFENDANT: Yes.

THE COURT: The plea letter does reserve to both sides the right to invoke the provisions of Federal Rule of Criminal Procedure 35, and to appeal if necessary, but that applies to applicable mandatory minimums or maximum sentences under the law.

Mr. Sweatt, I've gone over with you the guidelines and the stipulations that you have reached. I have also told you that the Government reserves the right to pay attention to your conduct up until sentencing, and that they might withdraw their agreement to an acceptance of responsibility adjustment under the federal guidelines.

In addition, if they think that you do anything between today and sentencing that amounts to an obstruction of justice, or is a new offense, they not only might oppose an acceptance of responsibility downward adjustment, but they may also ask me to move higher on the guideline scale because of it.

Once again, if that should happen, we'll have a hearing at which I will hear fully from both sides and then I will decide what to do about it under the advisory guidelines. Once again, please tell me that you understand that no matter what decisions I make at the time of sentencing, you will not be allowed to withdraw your guilty pleas that you have entered here today. Do you understand that?

THE DEFENDANT: Yes.

THE COURT: In addition, the parties have agreed that given the mandatory life sentence to which the defendant is subject under this agreement, the States Attorney's Offices in Prince George's County and Montgomery County, Maryland, and the Commonwealth Attorneys Offices in Fairfax County, the City of Alexandria, and Arlington County in Virginia, agree not to prosecute the defendant for the offense conduct set forth in Attachment A.

You understand that in addition to the agreements you have here with the Prosecutors in Federal Court, that the authorities in those jurisdictions that I just read have agreed that you will not be prosecuted there for the conduct that is set forth in that Statement of Facts. Do you understand that?

THE DEFENDANT: Yes.

THE COURT: Have we talked about today, here in court, all of the promises that you think make up your agreement with the Government?

THE DEFENDANT: Yes.

THE COURT: Other than what is written down in this document, in exhibit one that we have been reviewing, has anybody made any promise to you to convince you to plead guilty?

THE DEFENDANT: No.

THE COURT: Have you been threatened in any way?

THE DEFENDANT: No.

THE COURT: How many times did you meet with Mr. Chamble to talk about your decision to plead guilty and the terms of this plea agreement?

THE DEFENDANT: Once.

THE COURT: One time? Was that a very long meeting?

MR. CHAMBLE: One moment.

THE COURT: Mr. Chamble.

THE DEFENDANT: I'm sorry, Your Honor. I gave you the wrong information.

THE COURT: How many times have you met with Mr. Chamble to talk about your decision to plead guilty and to go over the terms of the plea agreement?

THE DEFENDANT: Four times.

THE COURT: Four times. Was that in person, he came to see you?

THE DEFENDANT: Yes, Your Honor.

THE COURT: Did he have the time that you thought was necessary to talk with you about this case?

THE DEFENDANT: Yes.

THE COURT: Has he answered all of your questions?

THE DEFENDANT: Yes.

THE COURT: Are you satisfied with the help that he has provided you?

THE DEFENDANT: Yes.

THE COURT: Counsel, what have I forgotten to ask or left unclear? Ms. Raman?

MS. RAMAN: Nothing from the Government, Your Honor.

THE COURT: Any of the other Government officials?

MS. ANDERSON: No.

THE COURT: Okay. Mr. Chamble, anything else?

MR. CHAMBLE: The Court was very comprehensive. There is nothing else.

THE COURT: Mr. Sweatt, understanding the charges that we've gone over, the applicable mandatory minimum sentences that apply, as well as the possible maximum sentences, the requirements that certain of these sentences be imposed consecutive to each other, and all of the rights that you will be giving up by pleading guilty, is it still your desire to plead guilty to all of these charges?

THE DEFENDANT: Yes.

THE COURT: I'm satisfied, Mr. Sweatt, that you do understand what it means to plead guilty; that mean that your pleas are being entered knowingly. I'm satisfied that you're pleading guilty based upon the written plea agreement, that there has not been any improper promise and there has been no threat. That means that these pleas are being entered voluntarily.

I am also satisfied, after hearing the stipulated facts, that there is an adequate factual basis for these pleas. Accordingly, I accept your pleas of guilty. You are as of now adjudged guilty of the offenses set forth in the three Informations that I read to you at the beginning of these proceedings.

We need to set a date for sentencing and request the preparation of a Presentence Report. Counsel, is the date of September 12 at 9:30 in the morning an appropriate date to set?

MR. CHAMBLE: Fine, Your Honor.

MS. RAMAN: Yes.

THE COURT: Mr. Sweatt, I've signed an order that sets sentencing for September 12 at 9:30 in the morning. More importantly, this order requests the Probation Office to prepare a Presentence Report. Mr. Chamble will help you provide some background information to the Probation Office to put in the report, and when a draft is ready, you'll review it with Mr. Chamble so you can let us know if there is anything that's inaccurate or incomplete.

It's a very important document. I rely on it quite a lot in making sentencing decisions. It is also provided to the Bureau of Prisons and to any supervising Probation Officer, so they can help decide where someone should serve a sentence and what programs are most appropriate for him.

I think it is in your interest that we make the report complete and accurate, so I urge you to cooperate in the process of its preparation. Assuming we have the information that we need and the proper amount of time set aside, we will have sentencing, and it is currently now scheduled for September 12 at 9:30 in the morning. Is there anything further this afternoon in Mr. Sweatt's case?

MS. RAMAN: Nothing from the Government.

THE COURT: Anything else? Mr. Chamble, anything further?

MR. CHAMBLE: Nothing from the defense, Your Honor.

THE COURT: All right. If not, thank you. That will complete the proceedings.

Appendix 3

Transcript of Sentencing: September 12, 2005

UNITED STATES OF AMERICA
VS.
THOMAS A. SWEATT

BEFORE THE HONORABLE DEBORAH K. CHASANOW

APPEARANCES:

ON BEHALF OF THE GOVERNMENT:
MYTHILI T. RAMAN, ESQ.
JAMES M. TRUSTY, ESQ.
ASSISTANT US ATTORNEYS

ON BEHALF OF THE DEFENDANT:
JOHN CHAMBLE, ESQ.

THE COURT: Good morning. Please be seated. Ms. Raman.

MS. RAMAN: Your Honor, calling the case of United States of America v. Thomas Sweatt, criminal number DKC-05-0230. This matter comes before this Court this morning for a sentencing hearing. Mythili Raman and Jim Trusty on behalf of the United States, along with Jennifer Anderson of the US Attorney's Office in the District of Columbia. We're also joined by the two primary case agents, Scott Fulkerson and Thomas Daley from the ATF and, of course, the victims' families.

THE COURT: Mr. Chamble.

MR. CHAMBLE: Good morning, Your Honor. On behalf of Thomas Sweatt, John Chamble. Mr. Sweatt is here, as well as numerous members of his family.

THE COURT: Very good. I have received quite a lot of written information. I want to make sure, first of all, that counsel have received the same material.

The Presentence Report prepared for us by Mr. Lambert is dated August 23, 2005. That's the revised Presentence Report, and I was made aware of the correspondence that went from counsel to Mr. Lambert prior to that document.

I have received letters from counsel concerning various issues that are pending and I went over with counsel before we came into court, and I'm sure each has seen the other's submissions.

In addition, both from the Probation Office and directly from the US Attorney's Office, I have received a number of Victim Impact Statements, and I understand, Ms. Raman, that there are more coming in since I was last provided copies, and that you will be providing them to me this morning.

MS. RAMAN: Yes, Your Honor.

THE COURT: Okay. I believe that's what I have received in writing, and I have reviewed all of that and we have some matters to hear this morning. Again, as I discussed with counsel, we thought we would begin by hearing from the members of the victims and victims' families.

MS. RAMAN: Your Honor, the first victim who would like to speak and address the Court is Carolyn Jones.

THE COURT: Good morning.

MS. JONES: I'm Carolyn Jones, the daughter of Lou Jones, and I have some pictures for you, Your Honor.

MS. RAMAN: I can hand them up to the Court.

THE COURT: Thank you.

MS. JONES: Okay. In order to tell you of the impact of this heinous crime have had on my family, I must first take you on a trip down memory lane. On August 29, 1916, in Hollister, North Carolina, Lou Edna White was born. She led an average life as a farm girl. At age eighteen, which is the first picture you have, Lou, who was a beautiful young woman, married a handsome young man of twenty years old from Rocky Mount, North Carolina, Ned Jones. They moved to Washington, DC, soon afterward.

Over the next seventeen years, Ned and Lou had three children: Eddie, Darlene, and Carolyn. When Carolyn was two and a half years old, they purchased a big house, which you also have a picture of the house pre-fire, at 2800 Evarts Street NE.

During the next four years, they had two more children, Sharon and Gloria. Ned worked in the construction field as a cement finisher until his death in 1974. Lou worked for the federal government at the Bureau of Engraving and Printing, where she retired in 1973.

Throughout the fifty years Lou lived in the home, she made from the house she bought in 1953. She went from being just Lou to becoming "Momma Lou," as this loving, caring woman provided a home for many family members and friends who needed a place to stay.

She fed anyone who showed up hungry. She befriended the lonely, comforted the broken hearted. She imparted her wisdom to all who asked. She worked diligently in her yard, planting and tending flowers all around the house.

She was an outstanding, hardworking member of her home church, New Southern Rock Baptist Church. Lou's ongoing personality took her many places, as she loved to travel, and in fact had just purchased a new car in May.

She had severe arthritis in both knees, causing her to walk slowly with a cane or a walker, but she didn't let it stop her. She had just decided to have her knees replaced to go with her new car, saying she was going to be hard to keep up with for sure.

What impact has the death of Lou Jones' life caused? The world has lost a vibrant, energetic, beautiful, loving, caring person, and we, Eddie, Darlene, Carolyn, Sharon, and Gloria, have lost our best friend, our confidant, our first love, our mother.

As a result, Eddie and Darlene have been hospitalized with heart-related problems, Carolyn and Sharon have been put on blood pressure medication, and Gloria has lost touch with everyone.

Ms. Sweatt sat in the courtroom when we were here before,

throwing kisses to Thomas as though he were a celebrity of sorts, when the truth of the matter is he is a vicious murderer who singlehandedly terrorized the Washington, DC, area, destroying property, and devastating lives for over two years.

Because of Mr. Sweatt, we no longer have the ability to hug, kiss, talk to, or touch our mother. All we have are our memories of her and a few pictures. And I would like to read this poem that was read at her funeral service:

If Tomorrow Starts Without Me

"If tomorrow starts without me and I am not there to see, if the sun should rise and find our eyes all filled with tears for me, I wish so much you wouldn't cry the way you did today while thinking of the many things we didn't get to say.

"I know how much you love me, as much as I love you and each time that you think of me, I know you'll miss me, too. But when tomorrow starts without me, please try to understand that an angel called my name and took me by my hand and said my place was ready in heaven far above, and that I'd have to leave behind all those I dearly love.

"But as I turned to walk away a tear fell from my eye, for all my life I'd always thought I didn't want to die. I had so much to live for, so much left to do, it seemed almost impossible that I was leaving you.

"I thought about the yesterdays, the good ones and the bad. I thought of all the love we shared and all the fun we had. If I could relive yesterday, just even for a while, I'd say good-by and kiss you, and maybe see you smile.

"But then I thoughtfully realized that this could never be, for emptiness and memories would take the place of me. And when I thought of worldly things I might miss come tomorrow, I thought of you and when I did my heart was filled with sorry.

"But when I walked through heaven's gates, I felt so much at home, when God looked down and smiled at me from his great golden throne. He said this is eternity and all I have promised you, today your life on earth is passed, but here your life starts anew.

"I promise no tomorrow, but today will always last and since each day is the same way, there is no longing for the past. You have been so faithful, so trusting and so true, but there were times that you did some things that you shouldn't do. But you have been forgiven and now at least you're free, so wouldn't you come and take my hand and share my life with me.

"So when tomorrow starts without me, don't think we're far apart, for every time you think of me, I'm right here in your heart."

And that's the only thing we have of our mother, just our memories, because we lost what meant the most to all of us. Thank you.

THE COURT: Thank you.

MS. RAMAN: Your Honor, Darlene Lloyd, who is another daughter of Ms. Edna Jones, Lou Edna Jones.

MS. LLOYD. Good morning.

THE COURT: Good morning.

MS. LLOYD: Yes. I'm the oldest girl of four, and I really didn't write anything down. I want to say a few things from inside my heart about Mr. Sweatt. Not only did he destroy this family, he destroyed a whole lot more families, homes and all, which our family home of over fifty years is now gone. We have just boards and a few shingles and everything burned, left over there of our home.

And I have a handicapped son, which was my mother's very first grandson. He is forty-two years old, and he still sits at the dinner table and asks me when Momma Lou is coming back. I kept trying to explain to him, there is no more Momma Lou.

When you sit and see his eyes full of tears, there is nothing you can do. I can wipe the tears away, but the pain is still in my son's heart.

And I have, like Carolyn said, I was hospitalized behind the passing of my mother. I will say my mother, but it's our mother. They found a problem, which mostly is my nerves down in my throat. I have trouble swallowing; food hangs up in my throat. I was so stressed out they gave me another cardiac catheterization to see how big a hole, if the hole had got bigger in my heart that I was born with.

And it's so many memories that I have of her, and I could go on and on. Although Mr. Sweatt has life, it would take his life, my life, and probably your life, to tell you all the good things about my mother.

I can remember one time when I was in the hospital, the doctor had given up on me, and it was about 2 in the morning. I opened my eyes and my mother was sitting beside the bed, reaching for my hand. She kept telling me, "You have a lot to live for. Think about your son."

She says, "I'm getting up in age. He's picky about his food. Nobody can feed him but you; nobody can buy clothes but you. You have a lot to live for." And I was in so much pain, I said I just want God to take me home. And, like I said, the doctors had given up, and she talked and talked and talked. And so when the nurse came in to take the vital signs, the temperature was down. It was all from the love of a mother sitting beside her child to keep her in this world and I'm here today, I'm living proof that my mother saved my life, her and God.

Then there was another...well, there was so many times. There was another time, when my father was living. He had a thing with collard greens. He and my mother would grow collard greens in the yard and I would cook them. And when I married I moved to South East, and every Sunday my mother had to drive my father to my house, just to get a plate of collard greens. She loved him dearly and when he passed, there was a big hole left in her heart.

She filled so many of us, because our grandmother lived there with us, and when my grandmother passed, my mother became my mother and my grandmother. Then, when our father passed, she was our mother, grandmother, and father.

She took the place of everybody, and she did so much for us. And although Mr. Sweatt has been charged with two murders, or deaths, he has committed three but he was only charged with two.

So, like I said, he's committed three murders, but he has only been charged with two. And what we have inside our mind, the memories, he can never take from us. We have T-shirts, and I had a thing where I always believed in giving a person flowers while they're here to enjoy. I have always given my mother flowers for the yard, mums, just flowers.

And I had to go buy flowers for my mother that she never did see, and she never could smell. When I had to go, my feet were so heavy; to have the arrangement made up to put on her casket, which I knew she could never see. And I wonder, 2004, Mother's Day, what was Mr. Sweatt doing? Did he call his mother on the phone? Did he visit her? Did he send her flowers?

Mother's Day for us was taking flowers to the cemetery, which I haven't been out there since we left my mother, because I can't go right now. It's still too soon, although it was in '03, but it just tears me up, knowing that's where I left my mother. And I will never see that smiling face, never feel her arms back around me, never taste no more of her food, which she cooked a lot and we ate a lot over her house. No more outings.

And I think another thing that stressed me out quite a bit when my birthday comes around, every year she would send me a card, and I have a card that she sent, a belated birthday, and she wrote, "Mom, and I'm sorry I forgot." That's the kind of person she was.

She would tell us she was sorry for something, which she was the mother. We should have been saying we're sorry for this, that, and the other. And the last card I received was April, '02, and I was in the hospital. April, '03 on my birthday. Like I said, it's a lot of aggrievement and it's a lot of hurt now, and it's still a lot of tears that will flow every day of my life and my siblings, and my mother's friends for her, because church, when I go to the church, I can still picture her casket sitting in the front of the church.

It was a long time before I could go back to that church, because it's a family church, and she's been a member, she was a member for over fifty years at this church.

Her children, we were baptized there. My children were baptized there. My daughter's two sons were baptized there, so it's like a family church, and the family will be there, but she is just not there no longer.

And I don't want to take all day because, like I said, I can go on and on and on about different things for my mother and what happened to her, because after what happened to my mother I was in fear of going out, because I didn't know who this person was or if it was more than one person. I was actually scared to go out in the street, because I said, "Well, if they went and did this to my mother, do they know where the rest of the family lives at?"

It was something to think about. Did they know where we all were at? And to stay in the house, I lost money from not working. I have bags under my eyes from not sleeping, because when I went to bed I did well if I slept one hour per night. And when I received a call that day that they actually had the serial arsonist for sure this time, I almost cried a river of tears. I have some relief.

I still do not sleep a full night, and I often wonder why Mr. Sweatt did this. Has he been able to just lay down in bed and sleep with nothing on his mind? I wonder, although he picked houses at random, if he was in the street at 4 in the morning, how did he just pick this particular house at random, when he sat on that porch for fifteen minutes? What was running through his mind beside he did want to set that porch on fire? And he was bold enough to sit there with that big porch light that she kept on the front and on the back, not knowing if the paperboy would come by and see him sitting there, and he's sitting there with his chemicals to set the house on fire.

Then I wondered by him working at Kentucky Fried Chicken, could he have known one of my nephews that used to hang down there? Could he have propositioned them, drove them home one night, came back? Then, you ask yourself, did he want to get caught? Was he actually tired of setting fires?

Although he didn't take every life from where he sat a fire, but he took enough when he did Ms. Anna Brown and my mother, known as Momma Lou, and my dear, beloved Aunt Gervis, that grieved herself to death right after my mother. Did he actually think that it could be my mother? Did he actually think that?

If he was stressed out, he has his mother. Did he realize that he was taking somebody's mother from them? He knew someone was in that house, 4 or 4:30 in the morning, with a porch light on, the cars were sitting in the back yard.

I just don't really know. And I said, I wonder if he could go back to that morning of June 5, 2003, would he have second thoughts about resetting this house on fire, or follow his first mind and pick his gas or whatever up and just walk back down the walkway, the same way he came up.

And I wonder also, which I thought I could ask him questions, if he could answer, but it's all right. I'll just direct them to you. Where did he go after he set this house on fire? Did he go down the street to the job? Did he go across the street and watch the flames or wait for the fire trucks to come? And I also wonder, when the house first start flaming, did he hear my mother, my little niece scream, and ask and beg for help?

My mother, like Carolyn stated, had arthritis very bad on both knees. She was able to get out the bed that morning, and it was so much smoke, I guess she got turned around, because she couldn't see the door or the two windows, because the firemen told me they found her laying at the foot of her bed, which they picked her up and laid her across his shoulder, like you would do a bag of potatoes. And when he started out her back-bedroom window he accidentally dropped our mother on the porch, the top, the room she had it on, and she fell off his shoulder on the roof.

And I wonder did that fall break her neck, because I know she was deceased when they brought her out from the smoke. I hate to think about it. I haven't seen the pictures. When they brought our mother out, both of her feet was burned off her legs. I wonder did he realize she was trying to run, but she lost both of her feet in the fire, trying to get out of that burning room, which she never did make out.

And then I wonder, how have his nerves been? Are they good, bad, or do he have a nervous condition? Is he taking any type of nerve medication from everything he has done, for the years he was the serial arsonist. So I'm not going to even go on with the rest of the questions I wanted to ask because, like I said, I don't want to take all day, and I would like for other people to get up and speak how they feel from the heart, and this is just some of what I feel.

And now, when I go home today and my son, the van brings my son back, and I turn the TV on every afternoon for the news, I will have to show him, there's Mr. Sweatt again, who did that to your grandmother, which this morning he left out the door again with tears because the news was on about today up in court, and I said, "There's Mr. Sweatt." They showed my mother's picture.

He said, "There's Momma Lou." I said, "Yes. Momma Lou is only on the TV. Momma Lou won't be back." So he left out this morning going to Melwood, his program. They furnish him with Melwood T-shirts to let them know when they out working they're from Melwood. But he didn't wear a Melwood shirt today.

He wore his Momma Lou shirt to work with him today. I said, "You carry your grandmother with you. She will forever be in your heart. Mr. Sweatt took your grandmother, known as Momma Lou, but he can't take her out of your heart, my heart, or anyone else's heart ever again." So we will have memories the rest of our lives about our mother, Momma Lou. Thank you.

THE COURT: Thank you.

MS. RAMAN: Your Honor, the next victim who would like to speak today is Ms. Anita Kyler.

MS. KYLER: Good morning.

THE COURT: Good morning.

MS. KYLER: I'm Jane Kyler, Anita Kyler's daughter. My mother sits here in the wheelchair. She's ninety-four years old. At the time of the incident she was ninety-two. I just wanted to say that my life has completely changed since the incident of the fire in March of 2003.

My mother normally sleeps down in the basement, where the fire occurred that particular morning. It just so happened one of the friends of the family, which is a play daughter, decided she wanted to spend the night. My sister was there with her, but my mom's play daughter wanted to spend the night that night, so she decided to sleep upstairs with her play daughter instead of staying downstairs.

Had she been down in the basement, she would have died also, because she cannot walk without some help. Therefore, when my mother's play daughter smelled smoke, she decided to come down—the fire alarm, the fire detector went off, so she came downstairs and opened the basement door and it was full of smoke, and she decided to run outside and get some help.

There was some gas, people in the car sitting in the car, so she went and got them to come back into the house to help her with my mom, to carry her out. She was sent to the hospital with smoke inhalation.

She...after that incident, she went to stay with my sister. One of my sisters, there are ten children in the family, ten of us. It was eleven. My younger sister died about four years ago from breast cancer.

So that night my mom—that morning, my mom had to go and stay with one of my sisters. So she stayed there for a few days because my sister works. So then she went to another sister's house, and she stayed there for a little while. After that we moved into an apartment on Taylor Street and stayed there for about six, seven months, and left there and she went back to my sister's house. Stayed there for a little while until we moved to St. Paul Senior Living Apartments, so we're there now, so she has been moved five times.

So this has been a very inconvenient thing, very depressing, stressful thing for both of us, not only for her and also the family. It has not been easy. I had to leave my house to come stay with her. I...she needs care twenty-four hours a day. I cannot leave unless there is someone there with her, fear that she might fall or try to get out of the chair, and she cannot just walk on her only, whereas before she could walk on her own at the house before the fire.

I can't travel like I used to because I'm unable to get someone to stay with her twenty-four hours for five to seven days a week. I can't go to the grocery store, doctors, church, or anywhere unless someone is with her. I can't go out with my friends and stay for a long period of time, because my sisters or brothers give me a time limit.

I didn't have time to exercise or go shopping. My mother gets depressed and starts crying because she wants to go back in her house, however it is not completed because of so many problems with the contractor and different things have been happening to the house, like roof repairs, porch and plumber work, and a whole bunch of things, and it has been like a roller coaster, ups and downs.

My mom has already depleted all of her savings trying to keep the house intact, just numerous repairs. And where she is living now, she has to pay $800 a month plus gas and electric, which runs quite high at times, and cable.

When the incident first happened she didn't want to go back to her house, but now she says she wants to go back. So she just goes back and forth. She wants to go. She doesn't. So she has mixed feelings about it. And then she was saying, "Well, why shouldn't I go? Stay here and paying all this rent when I have my own house."

However, you know, it's just one thing after another. She said she feel like an airplane, going from place to place and nowhere to stay.

And this is my mom's impact statement: "As the first known victim of the DC arsonist, I have suffered the longest. Since March 2003, I have been in a state of mental devastation and feel little hope of recovering. The changes in my life and my family lives since the event seem to be endless.

"To start with, like an airplane, I feel like I have been flying around, going from place to place, just trying to find a home of peace. I have uprooted my daughter from her home to live with me and help me through my struggles.

"And with over two years of bearing my burdens, this tragic event has taken a toll on her. She has endured several strokes but still continues to try to take care of me. Other family members have to bear the burden to help out by providing me with food, lodging, meals, and comfort, but none of that is the same when you are forced out of your home out of fears.

"No matter how pleasant my surroundings seem, it's never pleasant with fear in the mist. Then, as time goes on, your fear sometimes turn to rage, but you have felt...but you feel helpless knowing there is nothing you can do.

"Virtually incapacitated due to health reasons; all I could do was sit or lie down and cry. The world seems unsafe as long as the DC arsonist was still out there. For many of those months, going out socially was not on option, and nor should it be for him.

"This creature of society should not be allowed to walk around this city any more. He should forever be confined and treated accordingly. I have no mercy for this soul, and he should never be able to rest in peace."

My question, Judge, to the defendant, is to ask him why he did it. I would love to know exactly what made him do what he did and why, especially by my mom being ninety-two years old, been in that house for over fifty years. She has never had any problems. Thank you.

THE COURT: Thank you.

MS. RAMAN: Your Honor, Patricia Lewis is the granddaughter of Annie Brown, who was the victim in the second fatal fire with which Mr. Sweatt has been charged. Although she does not want to speak in court, she wanted us to read her Victim Impact Statement to the Court, and this is one of those that were recently submitted to us.

She says as follows: "Your actions have left a huge void in my family. We haven't been the same. The day you set the fire was my birthday, so instead of spending the day with my mom and grandmother, having cake and ice cream, I spent the day in the emergency room at GW, being told that the woman who raised me may not make it through the night.

"I had to be strong for everyone while I found myself dying instead. She lived nine days after that and God took her home on Valentine's Day. She was one of the nicest people in the world. Even you would have liked her.

"My seventy-two-year-old mom was also in the house, and she had Alzheimer's. On the day my grandmother died, I took my mom to see her to say goodbye. I watched my mom that night sit on the side of the bed, hugging her pillow, crying. Her condition got worse and she could not understand where her mom was. So for two and a half years, I've had to explain her death over and over so my mom wouldn't try to leave the house and try to find her mother.

"I can't forget the look of disbelief in her eyes and the sadness she felt because she couldn't remember, or the hurt she felt because her mom left her. We were a small family of seven, and she was our rock.

"Even though she was ninety-one years old, I could not imagine my life without her. How I do celebrate my birthday without reliving what you did? How do I explain to people why I cry on Valentine's Day?"

Your Honor, those were the victims who wanted to be heard today in court. Of course, the Court has received many other Victim Impact Statements. We've conveyed to the victims that the Court has read all of those submissions.

THE COURT: I certainly have, more than once. Okay. In order to proceed, the Court needs to adopt the proposed guideline findings that are set forth in the Presentence Report. It's my understanding that while those findings are not exactly identical to those that the parties had stipulated to, they are fairly close and that neither side wishes to take exception to the proposed findings. Is that correct, Ms. Raman?

MS. RAMAN: That's correct, Your Honor.

MR. CHAMBLE: That is correct, Your Honor.

THE COURT: All right. I have reviewed them and agree that they are correctly determined. These are advisory guidelines, both concerning the federal crimes and those transferred here from the District of Columbia.

I don't know that I need to state expressly what the guidelines are for each of the counts, but I will adopt the proposals as set forth in that Presentence Report.

Are there any other—there is one correction, a typographical error only in paragraph 18. It was the same typographical error that was initially in the Statement of Facts. It needs to be corrected, it's page seven. The name of the victim is misstated, but that was the only typographical error that I saw in here. Does anyone else have any issues with regard to the contents of the Presentence Report?

MS. RAMAN: Not from the Government, Your Honor.

MR. CHAMBLE: Not from the defense, Your Honor.

THE COURT: Okay. Ms. Raman, does the Government have any other factual information to bring to my attention before we proceed?

MS. RAMAN: No factual information, Your Honor. I think at some point we'd like to be able to express to the Court some of the other sentiments expressed by the victims who have either written or not written to the Court. But we would ask that the Court impose the sentences that we outlined in the September 7, 2005, letter to the Court.

THE COURT: Mr. Chamble, any other factual information you want me to be aware of?

MR. CHAMBLE: None, Your Honor.

THE COURT: No. All right. Then, Ms. Raman, I'll hear from you.

MS. RAMAN: Your Honor, as set forth in our letter dated September 7, 2005, it is clear that the parties have agreed that Mr. Sweatt should be sentenced to a mandatory life term of imprisonment, and I think all parties and the Court understand that that is a certainty and that Mr. Sweatt will be facing the rest of his life in court—in jail.

The victims that we heard today have very eloquently described what they personally suffered. Other victims have written to the Court and to defense counsel to describe the harms that they suffered over the last several years, and yet others weren't even able to find the words to write to the Court.

But all of those victims—the ones that spoke, the ones that didn't write, the ones that did write—have a unifying theme in their concerns and something they want to be conveyed to the Court, and that is that they have lost something.

In the cases of Ms. Jones' family and Ms. Brown's family, they have permanently lost a loved one. In the case of most of the victims, they have lost their financial security. We saw in some of the Victim Impact Statements that even those homeowners who had some insurance were not ever made whole financially. Some lost their insurance. Some asked for charity, charitable contributions, and were denied, so they lost their financial security.

Many of them lost their homes. They had to either live in hotels or motels temporarily. Some lost their home all together and have still not moved back to the homes that were damaged by Mr. Sweatt.

And, of course, all of them conveyed a feeling of losing their sense of personal security. Many spoke poignantly about the fact that they are simply not able to sleep at night, that their children still dream about the night that their house was set on fire, and that they simply don't have the same sense of security in their neighborhoods that they had before Mr. Sweatt crimes. And it is because of those victims that we believe that a sentence of life imprisonment is appropriate in this case.

There is just one thing that I think the Government wants to make clear to the Court, and that is that we feel the need to correct Mr. Sweatt's assertion in the probation report, presentence report, that he somehow didn't have control over what he did.

I think his actions over a number of years showed that he had choices at every juncture, and at each juncture he chose to set fires instead of stop. When he realized that he had set fatal fires, even the realization that he could permanently take someone's life away did not stop him.

When he sat on Ms. Jones' porch and sat for fifteen minutes, he had a choice but he chose not to stop himself, instead to set a fire. When he understood that he was the target of a serial arson task force and that sketches were being released of him and that a full-blown investigation was being launched, he did not stop and instead he played a game of cat and mouse with investigators.

And for all those reasons he was a danger to this community for several years and frankly continues to be a danger if he is ever released, and that is why the mandatory term of life imprisonment is warranted here, and we ask the Court to impose that sentence.

THE COURT: Mr. Chamble.

MR. CHAMBLE: Thank you, Your Honor. Your Honor, for the most part I agree with the Government's allocution, however we do take exception to their take that my client did not have a choice, or that he had a choice and he chose to do these things, because I have given both the Court and the Government a report that clearly says he did not have a choice, that he was laboring under a psychological compulsion.

And so where that is coming from is beyond me. But I'm not here today to debate with the Government choice or lack thereof. We're here today because Mr. Sweatt has brought us here today, by his actions and by his words.

Your Honor, we have read all of the Victim Impact Statements from Mr. Frederick Ackiss, Emily Brown, Gaston Brown, Florencianette Cooper, Joel Ehrlick, Denise Giles, Minnie Hodges, Mary Johnson, Gene Richardson, Adam Jordon, Carolyn Jones, Markos Kebede, Anita Kyler, Darlene Lloyd, Claudia McClennon, Ida McCoy Collins, Bettie Palmer, Tyrone Randall, Mark Reid, LaVerne Smith, James Thomas, LaQuanda Wilson.

And I'm here today on behalf Mr. Sweatt to let these victims who have written to the Court, to me, and those who have not written, that Mr. Sweatt understands the pain and havoc that he has brought on these lives. But I don't want people to lose sight of the fact that there is another victim here, and that is my client, Mr. Sweatt.

Mr. Sweatt's family that's in this courtroom today, they are victims. They are victims of a mental illness that Mr. Sweatt has labored with for many, many years, and hopefully he will get the attention and treatment that he so desperately needs.

Now, when one reads the victim impact statement, one cannot help but be moved by the loss and displacement, the psychological scars. What Mr. Sweatt has wrought upon these victims is not unlike the victims from Hurricane Katrina—people displaced from their homes, people living in cars, people losing jobs, people scarred physically, mentally.

We understand. We get this. But the real question, Your Honor, is what caused this terrible event? Hurricane Katrina was an act of nature. Mr. Sweatt's conduct was an act of mental illness, a psychological compulsion. A man who himself, prior to the involvement of his lawyer, and the Government's own evidence will attest to the fact that Mr. Sweatt struggled with this illness, was remorseful, was contrite.

It was Mr. Sweatt who, like a man, stood up and accepted responsibility for what he did, Your Honor. And rather than go through a lengthy trial and prolong the pain and suffering of these victims, he accepted responsibility, knowing that he would be serving himself up on a silver platter to a life sentence without the possibility of release.

That takes courage, that speaks to the true character of Mr. Sweatt when he is not under the influence of the mental illness that compelled him to commit these crimes, and we should respect that and we should honor that.

Mr. Sweatt not only accepted responsibility, walking into a life sentence, but he met with Government agencies to try to resolve other questions they had about fires. So he has done all that one can expect one to do under his circumstances, because he is truly remorseful.

It's enough to say, "I'm sorry." He has put actions to words, Your Honor. This is a tragic story. Mr. Sweatt, Your Honor, not unlike Robert Louis Stevenson's Dr. Jekyll and Mr. Hyde, this is a good man. He has lived a good life. This is not a criminally oriented person. This is a person that came from a stable, large family home with values, had an illness back then, managed to work and be productive, but there was a dark side to Mr. Sweatt that would take over, and that is why we're here today.

So you have the good Mr. Sweatt and you have the sick Mr. Sweatt, something that should have been treated, wasn't, will be. Regrettably, property and lives have been destroyed because of this sickness. But let us not hate the sinner. Hate the sin. Condemn the crime; do not condemn Mr. Sweatt, because this man is just as mortified as anyone about what he did under the cloud of that illness.

And this is not coming from whole cloth, Your Honor. Again, the Court has, and the Government has, documented medical evidence that speaks to why, why did he do this? It doesn't take a rocket scientist to figure out that this man is ill, and that illness is real, is tangible, and it's treatable.

And so, Your Honor, I ask the Court, in terms of where Mr. Sweatt is to serve the remainder of his days, that it be in a psychological facility designated by the Bureau of Prisons to treat this illness. Thank you.

THE COURT: Anything further from the Government before I turn to Mr. Sweatt?

MS. RAMAN: No, Your Honor.

THE COURT: Mr. Sweatt, this is now your opportunity yourself to tell me anything that you want me to know.

THE DEFENDANT: Thank you, Your Honor. Thank you, Your Honor. I'm glad for this day. To my victims and to the victims' families, I'm very sorry of all the harm that I have caused you.

To those who have lost loved ones, I share your hurt and I share your pain every day, so you're not alone, and I hurt every day. To the ones who come today with hate in their hearts, I ask God to replace the hate with understanding and that time will heal.

To my family, to my family, I'm sorry at the burden that I have put on you. I know it's a heavy burden, and I ask God to lift that burden and make your burdens light. For DC and Maryland and Virginia, God bless you all.

THE COURT: Mr. Sweatt is before the Court today for sentencing on fifteen separate counts. They arise in three different informations that were filed and consolidated in this court from Maryland, Virginia, and the District of Columbia.

The approach to sentencing has been consolidated as to all fifteen of the counts, and they will be discussed collectively.

At the outset, let me recognize that what the Governments have done in cooperating in this fashion is to select and charge certain offenses arising out of events that spanned several years, involved fires set at least forty-five different homes and to various automobiles as well.

The charges themselves do not reflect the full harm caused by and admitted to by Mr. Sweatt. They are, as I said, elected offenses. For a variety of reasons, the prosecutors elected to charge as they did. But they are in no way a complete articulation of the crimes that were committed, nor the extent of the harm.

In imposing a sentence on each of the counts, it is not intended to reflect necessarily the harm in that particular count. As I said, these were selected as appropriate substitutes, I guess, for charging the entirety. We would be here quite a long time if each offense, each event, was charged with all of the possible offenses. So we should look at the sentence as a whole, as a reflection of the harm and the crimes committed, rather than focus on any individual count in that sense.

One of the aspects of sentencing that the Government is seeking, appropriate on behalf of all the victims, is a restitution judgment. As part of the plea agreement Mr. Sweatt has agreed that the Court can impose restitution on all the offenses, whether charged specifically or not.

And while an effort was made to amass the information that would be necessary for the Court to make that determination in advance of today, we have not been successful in working out all of those numbers and all of the details.

As Ms. Raman has already intimated, it's been difficult for some of the people whose lives were affected to put even this type of information on paper in a reliable form. The law allows the Court to defer a final determination on restitution for a period up to ninety days after sentencing, and that's what I will do.

In addition, the statute we are working under, the Mandatory Victim Compensation, I'm not sure what the exact wording is, also limits the types of losses that are compensable in a restitution judgment. For property damage, the Court is limited to ordering return of the property or assessing restitution for any diminution in value. So for the property damage claims, we will be limited to the cost or repair or replacement of any property that was damaged or destroyed. Consequential damages are not appropriate in the context.

Bodily injury claims will include necessary medical and related services and can include lost income. There can be no restitution for lost income in connection with strictly property damage loss. Those people who were covered in some sense by insurance will not be receiving a direct reimbursement or restitution award for those amounts that were covered by insurance, although if claimed as a secondary restitution victim, perhaps an insurance company will get an award.

The restitution statute requires the Court to determine and impose a judgment of restitution without regard to a defendant's ability to pay. That does not mean that it will be collectable. Mr. Sweatt has no financial resources at present with which to pay any restitution, and as we will discuss in just a moment, he will not be in a position to earn income in the future of any significant amount, so it is entirely unlikely that there will be a collection on the restitution, but it will constitute a judgment against Mr. Sweatt and can appropriately remain as a judgment should his financial situation ever change.

But despite the fact that we will spend some time and get all of the information that any of the victims and the families want to submit, and I will enter a restitution judgment within the next ninety days. The reality is, and everyone needs to understand this, that this will not be a source of compensation, likely not.

I also want to recognize the cooperation and coordination of all of the law enforcement authorities, prosecutors, victim witness coordinators, who participated in this. Without their cooperation and energy, this case would not have been handled as well as it has been.

I have had the opportunity to read and now to hear the statements from some of the direct victims and some of the slightly more remote victims here. And, as Ms. Raman has said and Mr. Chamble echoed, they do speak eloquently on their behalf.

It is...Those of us who are participants in this, who have had an opportunity to read all of those statements, and each of you who submitted them only know your own words, except for those that were repeated here today. There are many who did not submit statements, either in writing or orally, and I want to assure you that from my perspective, those who did submit information spoke for everyone.

There were parallels, striking parallels, from those who did write and speak. There was fear. There was real, real fear, despite the knowledge they were told by law enforcement that whoever had committed this offense was acting at random and would not likely come back to the same place. So the fear that this particular person would do it again was intellectually known not to be realistic. The fear, the loss of the personal security, was expressed by everyone.

Many of you did some soul searching, wanted to know why. "Why were we the target? Did we do something to someone we don't know?" All of you were in some sense thinking there had to have been a reason, and we need to know what it was that somebody thought we did wrong. Well, you have your answer to that. There was no reason. It was at random. There was no particular purpose. Nobody who was a victim has done anything wrong.

Each spoke of the disruption to their lives. Each family in this case, as Mr. Chamble has suggested, has displacement and disruption equivalent to those faced by people on the Gulf Coast in the wake of Katrina. But in this case, each of you faced that displacement alone, without the larger community support that we are fortunately seeing expressed for those in the Gulf Coast area.

It was particularly alarming to me to read in the statements some of the lack of empathy that many of you faced from employers, from those Government and other service agencies who should have been in a position to help, whether charitable or otherwise. It was really shocking to me that so many of you had those kinds of difficulties, and I can only hope that the fact that we as a nation have gone through more of these collective tragedies, that we've learned and that we are more empathetic to those in our midst who suffer this kind of displacement in the future, and that we have learned, and that it won't be for others in the future.

All of you speak well of the law enforcement response. Welcoming the information that was provided to you and the help that was coming to you from the law enforcement community. All expressed concern that the person who was doing this to our community be stopped, and many of you did recognize that any person who could do this was seriously in need of help, because this couldn't be done by anyone in their right mind. And that those sentiments were expressed eloquently by all who wrote and all who spoke today, and I know they spoke not just for themselves but for everyone who was affected and, indeed, for all of us in the community because while you were the most directly affected by this, the overall fear of the community certainly went beyond those forty-five homes that were burned.

A special note, of course, to those who lost loved ones. There can be nothing that anyone can say that truly can ease the pain. I was very much taken by the fond memories that were expressed in the hearts of all of you, and our sympathies to you and your families.

The sentence that I will impose now will assure that Mr. Sweatt will not ever again walk free. It will take me some time now to work through each of the counts. It is my intention overall to impose concurrent sentences on the eleven counts that do not either statutorily or under the guidelines require consecutive sentencing.

All told, these sentences will amount to close to a sentence of life in prison plus 136 years. The sentences are as follows:

Mr. Sweatt, it is the judgment of the Court that on the Maryland information, you be sentenced on Count 1 to a terms of 262 months; Count 2, which carries a ten-year maximum, will be a sentence of 120 months, concurrent to Count 1. I will skip Count 3 for the moment. Count 4 is another 120 months, again a ten-year maximum count. Count 5 is a five-year mandatory minimum and a twenty-year maximum, and the sentence is 240 months, twenty years concurrent. Count is, again, a ten-year maximum count and that is 120 months, again concurrent.

On the Virginia information, Count 1 is a five-year mandatory minimum and a twenty-year maximum. Accordingly, the sentence is 240 months, concurrent to the others I have also announced. Count 2 is a seven-year mandatory minimum, a forty-year maximum, and the sentence is 262 months, which is the top of the guideline range determined under the federal sentencing guidelines.

In the District of Columbia, Count 1 is a five-year mandatory minimum and a maximum of twenty years. Accordingly, the sentence is 240 months concurrent. I'm skipping Count 2. Count 3 is a ten year—Counts 3 and 4 and 5 are each ten-year maximums, and its 120 months concurrent on all of those.

So that is the eleven counts for which the sentences are concurrent. The maximum is the 262 months. All of the others that are lesser sentences are concurrent to those.

On Count 3, in the Maryland criminal information, this count carries a thirty-year mandatory minimum sentence, and that must be consecutive to the other terms that have just—well, to the crime of violence to which it attaches.

I therefore impose a thirty-year consecutive sentence on Count 3 in the Maryland Criminal Information, consecutive to the 11 that I have just announced.

Count 2 in the District of Columbia, I will save again. I am now going to Count 6 for the District of Columbia sentence. This is, under the District of Columbia guidelines, a thirty-year minimum to a maximum of sixty years, which is what's considered a life sentence under the District of Columbia statutes. Count 6 is sixty years, consecutive to the 11 that were first announced and consecutive to Count 3 in the Maryland information.

Count 7 carries a maximum of forty years' imprisonment. The guideline, under the District of Columbia's newly adopted advisory guidelines, is either, it's 144 to 288 months, and it should be consecutive to all other sentences. Accordingly, the sentence on Count 7 is 288 months, and that is consecutive to the eleven first counts I announced, consecutive to Count 3 and consecutive to Count 6 of the DC charges.

Finally, Count 2 in the District of Columbia is a mandatory sentence of life in prison, and accordingly the judgment on Count 2 of the District of Columbia information is life in prison, and this is consecutive to all of the other sentences that I have just imposed.

As I calculate this, this is a life sentence plus almost 136 years in prison. I will recommend swift evaluation for any mental health issues in a medical facility and appropriate treatment once that evaluation is completed.

It is up to the Bureau of Prisons to make that determination, but I will provide to them the information that has been provided to me, and recommend that they follow up on it promptly.

Mr. Sweatt will spend the rest of his life in prison, but the law requires the Court to impose terms of supervised release with conditions, should that change, which it is not going to do. On the Maryland counts 1 and 3, the District of Columbia counts 2, 6 and 7, and the Virginia Count 2, supervised release are five years. On all of the other counts the supervised release will be three years. Supervised release will run concurrently on all of those.

Should we ever need to reach this, Mr. Sweatt will as a condition of supervised release participate in any mental health treatment program as directed by the Probation Officer.

I have already deferred the determination of restitution until we have all of our other information. Should there ever be release, Mr. Sweatt will continue to pay restitution based upon a schedule to be set, if that day should ever happen.

I will not impose any fine. As I have already stated, there is simply no financial resource from which to pay any fine. But I am imposing special assessments on each of the counts. This is money that does go into a fund to help people who are victims of crime, and for that reason have financial problems that they didn't otherwise have.

The special assessment will be $100 per count for a total of $1,500. That will be part of the judgment and can be collected, if possible, through the financial responsibility program of the Bureau of Prisons.

Mr. Sweatt waived his right to appeal all of my sentencing decisions, as did the Government, as part of the plea agreement, but let me advise you, Mr. Sweatt, that if you think you have the right to appeal any of the decisions that have been made, you would need to file that appeal in writing within ten days of today, so talk that over with Mr. Chamble very promptly, so he could assist you if that's what is needed to be done.

Have I neglected to discuss any aspect of sentencing that I need to?

MS. RAMAN: No, Your Honor.

THE COURT: Anything, Mr. Chamble?

MR. CHAMBLE: No, Your Honor.

THE COURT: Ms. Spence, anything from the Clerk's perspective?

THE CLERK: No, Your Honor.

THE COURT: Okay. Mr. Lambert, anything further?

PROBATION OFFICER: No, Your Honor.

THE COURT: All right. I hope today and the opportunity to speak and to understand that we have all heard everything is of some assistance to the victims, the victims' families.

Mr. Sweatt, I hear what you have said. You have appropriately, I think, pled guilty. Whatever you faced in terms of any problems cannot in any way justify the actions that you took. Actions that very really terrorized a community and impacted a great many number of lives.

If appropriate, there will be treatment available for you in the prison system, but regardless, you will spend the rest of your life in a prison system so that you cannot ever again affect anyone else's life in this drastic way.

I will prepare and enter the judgment in writing, and I will get copies out to everyone. Given the issues, it may take the Bureau of Prisons some time to make an appropriate designation. Once that has happened, you will be transferred from your current detention facility. Is there anything further from any one?

MS. RAMAN: Not from the Government, Your Honor.

THE COURT: No. If not, thank you. We'll stand adjourned.

ACKNOWLEDGMENTS

1) First and foremost, I would like to thank God.

2) Without the love and support of my wife, Carrie, this book would have never been completed. You are my backbone, my best friend, and number one supporter. You have always believed in me.

3) I am very thankful for the support of my immediate family during this endeavor.

4) I could write an entire page expressing my gratitude and thanks for the help and support of a great friend, Dr. Burton A. Clark. I owe so much to you, not only for your help with this book, but also for your guidance throughout the years. The opportunities you have given me are remarkable. You will receive the first two tickets to the movie premiere. Thank you for everything.

5) I am forever grateful for the guidance and direction from my good friend Fire Chief Dennis Rubin. You opened many doors and gave me opportunities that I would not have been able to receive on my own.

6) I owe a great deal of thanks to "R.S." She helped get things moving for me at jump street and provided me with valuable information that nobody else could have done for me. Without her, this book may have never begun. Thank you for sticking your neck out for me and believing in this "idea" from the beginning.

Have a book idea?
Contact us at:

info@mascotbooks.com | www.mascotbooks.com